DEV

DEVI DEVATA

DEVI-DEVATA

The Gods & Goddesses of India

Subhadra Sen Gupta

Rupa & Co

Published 2001 by
Rupa & Co.
7/16, Ansari Road, Daryaganj
New Delhi 110 002

Offices at:
15 Bankim Chatterjee Street, Calcutta 700 073
135 South Malaka, Allahabad 211 001
PG Solanki Path, Lamington Road, Mumbai 400 007
36, Kutty Street, Nungambakkam, Chennai 600 034
Surya Shree, B-6, New 66, Shankara Park,
Basavangudi, Bangalore 560 004
3-5-612, Himayat Nagar, Hyderabad 500 029

ISBN 81-7167-530-1

Typeset by
Nikita Overseas Pvt Ltd
19A Ansari Road
New Delhi 110 002

Printed in India by
Gopsons Paper Ltd
A-14 Sector 60
Noida 201 301

*The two finest storytellers in my family
who brought the devis and devatas to life
and made their myths a part of our lives.*

*In memory of my grandmother Tulsi Dasi Devi
and my mother Sucharita Sen Gupta who
is still telling the stories to the new generation.*

Contents

Introduction

A book on Hindu mythology may seem like an anachronism in today's world of digital communications and space travel. After all, while we explore the far reaches of the outer space, we fail to locate the heaven where our devis and devatas live. One wonders if there is any place for the ancient myths and legends in our lives and if the children growing up with computers will find these tales of the ancient battles of gods and demons interesting. But in fact, myths continue to fascinate both adults and children. They are a record of the creative imagination of a people and the literary heritage of a country.

The magic of myths is eternal. Even today comic books and television serials telling the stories of Shiva or Krishna are guaranteed to be popular because in addition to being a part of the people's faith, they are also great stories. These ancient tales continue to enrich our imagination and give our spiritual life both direction and meaning. For Indians, myths are not just relevant, they continue to be a vibrant part of their daily existence.

Myths have something to offer everyone. For children surrounding their grandmothers listening wide-eyed to the adventures of Durga battling the demons, they are fabulous tales. As adults they begin to question and probe, wondering why we worship Vishnu but have forgotten Brahma or seek the hidden meaning behind the myth of a celestial river's reluctant descent to earth. Because within their layers of magical happenings, myths often carry a kernel of truth, an ethical observation or even an echo of a true historical event. Myths have this intriguing habit of taking the history of a people and wrapping it up in clouds of magic, memory and mystery.

What is amazing about Hindu myths is the way they have remained alive in the minds of the people even today, when in most cultures they have receded into the pages of books. In India our gods and goddesses are living deities, receiving their daily puja at temples and their festivals are still celebrated with fervour. Indians have this ability to live at many levels, devotees holding puja flowers also carry their cell phones into temples, naked sadhus use video cameras at Kumbh Melas, and priests check their digital watches before drawing out astrological charts. There is this acceptance of the many aspects of life and so there is little sense of conflict between the traditional and the modern.

The Hindu world of deities and their myths have been gathered into this book for people who need a compact, easy reference to the complicated, intricate, and at times contradictory world of Hindu mythology. It tries to answer the questions that rise to our minds and also hopefully encourage readers to delve deeper into this living heritage by going back to the original sources in the Vedas and Puranas.

Most of the books written on Hindu myths were either scholarly studies or were aimed at children, where the myths were treated purely as stories. There was a need for a comprehensive study of myths for the lay readers and surprisingly the few I could find had been written over a century ago. This book is aimed at the readers of today, especially of the post-Independence generations of urban Indians who have grown up with a limited or fragmented knowledge of the myths and want to know more.

So this book not only narrates the myths but also tracks the evolution of Hindu mythology from the pantheon of Vedic deities to the Puranic trinity of Brahma-Vishnu-Shiva and the Devi. It delves into the growth of their powers and studies the rise and fall of the Vedic gods. The book also tries to clarify and organise the maze of myths and legends so that the story of Hindu mythology becomes easier to understand.

Even then, a journey into the world of Hindu myths can be a very confusing one. Our ancient books contain an immense collection of tales, often many versions of the same one and at times stories that contradict each other. The attributes of the deities change and merge and at times the same ones are claimed by many other gods. For instance, in the Vaishnava myths Vishnu has taken all the roles of creator-preserver-destroyer while the Shaiva myths credit them all to Shiva with Brahma apparently without any powers. Both Indra and Varuna are called king of heaven and both are invoked to give rain. If Indra is the commander of the army of the gods then so is Kartikeya. The difference between Kali, Chamunda. and Chandika is hard to comprehend.

So if readers disagree with the version of a story told here it just means their original source is a different one. One cannot create logic and order in a world that thrives on its myriad, ever changing colours. Similarly scholars may find this book elementary but there is a need for such reader friendly books on aspects of our heritage. This book is a result of the great work done by scholars and all that has been done is that their wisdom and knowledge has been gathered and presented in a more accessible manner, so that this fascinating heritage of our country can continue to enthrall our minds and spirits, adding colour, magic and a touch of the unexpected into our regimented lives.

CHAPTER ONE

The Great Shining Ones

"This is that truth. The sacrificial rites that the sages saw in the hymns are manifoldly spread forth in the three Vedas. Perform them constantly, O lovers of truth. This is your path to the world of good deeds.

When the flame flickers after the oblation fire has been kindled, then, between the offerings of the two portions of clarified butter, one should proffer his principal oblation—an offering made with faith..."

— Mundaka Upanishad

The puja is an eternally beautiful ceremony of worship. As the devotees gather at the door of the sanctum of a temple, the deity stands within, decorated with flowers, wearing silks, gold and jewels like royalty, anointed with sandalwood and vermilion. The air echoes to the rising chants of mantras, the blowing of conch shells, and the ringing of bells. The garbha griha is lit by golden oil lamps and perfumed by the rising smoke of incense as the priest lights the many flamed metal lamp for the ceremony of the aarti.

Then, as the chanting rises to a crescendo, the flickering points of flame are raised up to illuminate the benign face of the deity, drifting in and out of view through the lazily drifting smoke. The moving golden light catches the shimmer of silks, making the jewels glitter and the flowers glow with soft colours as the deity seems to smile a benediction on the people. In India, this worship has continued unchanged for many millennia. Unlike most countries where their mythology is only found in books, even today the gods and goddesses of the Hindu pantheon are a living and powerful presence in the lives of the people.

Since the dawn of time, every civilization has created its own pantheon of gods because humans seem to need their all seeing, all encompassing, omnipotent presence. All the questions of existence—of life and death, joy and sorrow, are directed to these divine, all knowing beings. And as these gods and goddesses are given faces, they gain their own characters and gather their own histories and their myths begin.

As the historian and novelist, Robert Graves writes, "Myth has two main functions. The first is to answer the sort of awkward questions that children ask, such as 'Who made the world? How will it end? Who was the first man? Where do souls go after death?'... The second function of myth is to justify an existing social system and account for traditional rites and customs." The omnipotent gods are propitiated with sacrifices and worshipped with rituals. Then temples are built for them and people take their hopes and prayers to these palaces of the gods.

All the inexplicable, fearful, and threatening things in the world had to be connected to the mysterious world of the gods. From the starry bowl of the night sky to the rising sun, the arrival of the monsoons with thunder and lightning to the strange destructive and beneficent powers of fire, earthquakes, volcanoes and cyclones. All the mysteries of nature and the magic of this earth had to be worshipped as gods because they made humans feel helpless before forces they could not control or predict. From the Egyptian sun god Ra to Poseidon, the Greek god of the sea, every civilization has created its first gods from the elements of nature.

The first images of gods and goddesses to be found in India have been traced back to the Indus Valley Civilization. The terracotta seals show a horned fertility god surrounded by animals, there are female figures of a Mother Goddess and they probably also worshipped sacred trees and animals. But we know little of the people of Mohenjodaro and Harappa, cities that flourished around 2500 B.C.E and the deities they venerated. What they were called, how they were worshipped, their myths and legends still remain a mystery. These gods and goddesses must have had names, rituals of worship, may be even temples but as long as their script remains undeciphered we cannot know more about these great deities.

Singing to the Gods

When the nomadic Aryan tribes of Central Asia swept into India from Persia they brought their own gods with them and the songs that they sang to their deities. The most precious literary and religious heritage of India is the Rigveda, a collection of 1028 hymns the Aryans sang to their gods. These hymns were probably composed between 1500 and

900 B.C.E and so the Rigveda is not only India's most sacred text, it is also the oldest piece of religious writing in the world. This and the three later sacred books—the Samaveda, the Yajurveda and the Atharvaveda are invaluable anthologies of sacred writing which provide us with all our knowledge of the gods and goddesses worshipped by the ancient Aryans.

The Rigveda is a simple collection of songs of praise to be sung during the sacrifices. The Samaveda rearranges these hymns for the priesthood to be used for liturgical purposes. The Yajurveda contains sacred chants and formulae to be used during sacrifices and the Atharvaveda consists of magical spells and incantations in the form of verses to be chanted.

The Aryans were nomadic herdsmen, wandering across the land in search of pastures. Such a life meant they did not build temples. For them worship of the gods was through performing yajna, with sacrifices at a sacred fire and the singing of sacred hymns of praise. It was very different from present day pujas with their elaborate rituals and myriad ceremonies. The object of the veneration of the Aryans were gods they called devas, 'the shining radiant ones'. Like the mythology of most ancient civilizations, the early gods, the devas of the Aryans were mostly aspects of nature—the sun, moon, sky or earth, thunder, lightning, and fire. And reflecting their aggressive, warlike culture all the important deities were warrior-males, the goddesses were of less importance.

The great father of the gods was a vague, formless deity called Dyaus who personified the heavens but he was not worshipped much. The active king of the gods who would listen to prayers and come to the rescue of his devotees was

Lord Indra. He was both a warrior-king and the god of the weather, especially of the rains. Like the Aryans who had conquered the land on their horse chariots, the warrior Indra led the gods to victory against their enemy, the demons. As the all powerful weather god Indra battled the evil demon Vritra who was holding on to the rains in the clouds and allowed the rains to fall to earth. Unlike the remote and inactive Dyaus, Indra was the energetic and beneficent king, who was the recipient of the largest number of hymns in the Rigveda. During battles, Indra rode out with Vayu, the god of the winds and the army of the Maruts, the gods of the storms, all ready for battle, singing martial songs.

Many aspects of the omnipotent sun received worship. There was Surya, the sun god, riding his seven horse chariot across the sky. Also Ushas, the goddess of dawn and the twin Ashvins who were the sacred horsemen. Pusan was also a sun god and so was Savitra, who was called the stimulator as he directed the sun. It is the active and energetic Savitra who has the most sacred hymn in the Vedas dedicated to him. The verses of the Gayatri Mantra sing the praises of Savitra and it is the mantra that is chanted all across the land even today. At dawn as the golden ball of the sun appears across the horizon, by river banks and temple doorways, people raise their faces to the beneficent rays of Surya and chant this exquisite mantra of thanksgiving,

> "Om bhur bhuvasya
> Tat Savitur varenium
> Bhargo devasya dhimahi
> Dhiyo yo na prachodayat."

O splendid and playful sun, we offer this praise to thee.
Enlighten this craving mind. Be our protector.
May the radiance of the divine ruler guide our destiny.
Wise men salute you with oblations and praise.

As the most important part of the rituals of the worship
of the Aryans was the lighting of the holy fire, the fire god
Agni was one of the most important gods. He was the god
of the priests because it was Agni who carried the sacrifices
from the humans to the gods. He was also the god of the hearth
as every home had its own fire. He could be found on earth
and in the sky as Agni also dwelt among the clouds as lightning.

The strangest of the Vedic gods was not an aspect of
nature but a drink called Soma. The hymns describe a potent
drink made from some unidentifiable plant that was drunk
during sacrifices. Drinking Soma led to hallucinations, a great
feeling of power, and a closeness to the gods. Scholars have
speculated about this mysterious plant and suggestions have
ranged from mushrooms to hemp that is still used to make
the intoxicating drink of bhang. Soma must have been a
powerful potion indeed as there is a delightful hymn in which
an inebriated Indra sings happily,

> "Like wild winds, the draughts have raised me up.
> Have I been drinking soma?
> The draughts have borne me up, as swift steeds a
>   chariot
> Have I been drinking soma?"

Indra, Agni, Savitra, and Soma were all benign gods but the
Aryans feared the powerful Varuna. He was second in power

only to Indra and possessed a moral authority and the power to punish that made his worshippers fearful. Varuna was a great king, not a boisterous warrior like Indra. He was the all-knowing deity who had his spies everywhere reporting to him on the actions of the people and like a king he passed judgement, meting out punishments. Varuna was the firm, humourless judge and one prayed to him with fear and trembling.

The other gods the Aryans feared were Yama, the Lord of the Dead and Rudra who was called the 'Howler' and was an angry, vengeful, red-faced god. The goddesses were minor deities but had some hymns dedicated to them. There was Prithivi, the Earth Goddess, Aditi, the Great Mother of the gods and Aranyani, the Lady of the Forest. Ushas, the goddess of dawn and Ratri, the goddess of the night must have appealed to the poets because they had some lyrical hymns in their praise.

The Gods of the Puranas

As the Aryan tribes moved eastward into the Gangetic plains they encountered more of the older tribes and the gods of the older Dravidian civilization of the Indus Valley. The Aryan caste system sprang from the wish to keep the two cultures separate but intermingling was a natural result of the two peoples living together. Dravidian women marrying Aryan men brought their own gods and goddesses into their new homes. As the Aryans settled down in villages they began to adopt the Dravidian system of worship, with temples and the rituals of puja. The old system of singing of hymns and the custom of sacrifices were also absorbed into the rituals performed in temples.

After the creation of the Vedas, newer religious and philosophical treatises were written that reflected this synthesis of two cultures. From the Upanishads to the Puranas and the epics of the Mahabharata and the Ramayan, the sacred books dealt not just with the gods and their rituals of worship but scholars now addressed deeper philosophical questions. And it is the Puranas, filled with tales of gods and goddesses that are the greatest source of Hindu mythology.

As temples were built, the priestly class of Brahmins rose in influence and prescribed their own rules for the worship of the deities in these temples. Slowly the nomadic tradition of sacrifices under an open sky was transformed into a religion with temples, priests, rituals, and festivals. Scholars differentiate between the two traditions by calling the original Aryan worship as Brahmanism and the later system as Hinduism.

As villages and towns rose, the economy became more agricultural, commerce developed, and the rhythm of the lives of the people changed. People now felt the need for newer gods. Also, the cult of the older Dravidian deities had remained a powerful presence in the lives of the people and now these deities were incorporated into the Hindu pantheon. Many of the older deities lost their influence and newer gods and goddesses rose to prominence.

By the time of the Puranas, written between the 4th to the 12th century AD the two most powerful deities were not Indra and Agni but Shiva and Krishna and what is intriguing is that they are both dark skinned gods, reflecting their ancient Dravidian lineage. This rise and fall of the deities is one of the most fascinating aspects of Hindu mythology. And the other interesting aspect is that the process goes on into the age of computers and space travel. For instance, an obscure goddess called Santoshi Ma suddenly rose to prominence in the latter half of the twentieth century mainly because of a popular film. Today her garish icon has found a niche beside all the ancient deities in the temples. Hinduism has this intriguing ability to accept and absorb change while allowing everything to endure in many intricate forms.

The old Brahmanical nature gods—Indra and the Maruts, Vayu, and Soma were worshipped less and less. The new pantheon that received prayers and had sacred books dedicated to them were those praised in the Puranas. Vishnu was a minor god in the Vedas, described as an aspect of the sun god Surya but it was Vishnu who rose to power, gathering within himself the aspects of many other minor deities. Then the legends of great kings and warriors were merged into his myths and the avatars of Vishnu included Rama and Krishna. By the reign of the Guptas, in the 4th and 5th century AD Vishnu had become a magnificent, many-faceted god with temples dedicated to this colourful, intricately imagined and utterly fascinating god. There is always some aspect of Vishnu that appeals to every worshipper, from the vengeful Narasimha to the compassionate Krishna and the dutiful and honourable Rama.

Shiva's rise to power is an even more interesting tale. There was no god called Shiva in the Vedas. The closest in qualities was the angry god called Rudra who was an aspect of the fire god Agni. In some hymns he is described with the word "shiva", which means auspicious. As a god who had absorbed many elements, Shiva is somewhat of a contradiction. He is both the supreme ascetic and a fertility god, a lord of the animals and a lord of the dance. Many of his aspects resemble those of the nameless god of the Dravidians we see on seals seated in a yogic posture, wearing horns, and surrounded by animals. Scholars speculate that the cult of this fertility deity must have been kept alive by the non-Brahmanic people and slowly the worship of Shiva became incorporated into the mainstream of society.

With the powerful presence of Shiva rose the worship of the Mother Goddess and her magical cults and subtle fertility mysteries. She became the consort of Shiva, called his shakti, the source of all his power and as her influence grew she gathered many aspects around herself. She was not just the loving wife and generous mother, she was also a warrior queen and a vengeful, merciless goddess battling demons. The appearance of Shiva and the Mother Goddess was a result of the growing influence of the Dravidian South where their cults had survived. The appeal of these two deities was much too powerful to be resisted by the Brahmanical priesthood.

During the Puranic times, the Hindu pantheon as we know it today, crystallised into a proper system of worship. We now had the great trinity of gods—of Brahma the creator, Vishnu, the preserver, and Shiva, the destroyer. And with them rose the Mother Goddess, in her many aspects as Parvati-Durga-Lakshmi-Saraswati. Appearing not just as the consort but also as a deity in her own right, with her own devotees. Bestowing wealth and knowledge, good harvests, and the power to combat and triumph over evil. The Aryan pantheon was slowly eclipsed from the minds of the people, Indra got no more hymns written in his praise, Agni received no temple and was only invoked during the sacrifices and mighty Varuna became a minor god of the waters.

The Hindu world of myths is like an intricately woven piece of silk. However, do not search for a logical pattern in it. At times the stories are contradictory, at others the same myth has different endings or is credited to different gods. If one myth claims the supremacy of one god, a second asserts the claims of another. Gods change their attributes and their powers wax and wane like the moon. However, at the end of it, all the threads merge to create a vibrant kaleidoscope of the Hindu imagination through the ages.

A Personal Communion with God

The Hindu gods are surprisingly human in character. They are not omnipotent, solemn, and judgemental supreme beings like the Semitic and Christian gods. They do not even expect absolute and unquestioning obedience like the god of Islam. Hindu gods are supremely powerful but they are also capable of impulsive mistakes, sudden anger, and great compassion. The devotees always have a personal image of the deity in their minds and the many hued gods match their spiritual needs. For the devotee of Shiva, the god is the benign but at times volatile father, our Baba Vishwanath. Vishnu can be the calm, royal Rama and also the more subtle, humorous, and kind Krishna, who is not just king but also the divine lover and a compassionate god. In her many aspects, the Mother Goddess as Parvati is gentle, as Annapurna she is generous, and as Durga fiercely protective of her worshippers.

The worship of the deities also reflects this personal bond between the god and his devotee. Hinduism has no tradition of congregational worship, each person prays directly to the deity. The Brahmin priest performs the ritual of puja at the temple but you can pray to your god anywhere—at home, by a river, under a tree. You do not need a priest to perform puja and the Hindu rituals of worship treat the deity as human. The idol is dressed in silk garments, garlanded with flowers, anointed with vermilion and sandalwood, welcomed with the lighting of lamps and the burning of incense, and offered food to eat. There is a personal and oddly touching rapport between the devotee and his god.

In the temple the god is the king of kings and the temple is his palace, so the rituals of puja resemble the anointing of royalty. In the most formal form of puja there are fifteen main rituals. The idol is offered a seat, the asana, in the sanctum and swagata, the welcome mantras, chanted. The feet are washed with a mixture of five ingredients—milk, yoghurt, ghee, sugar, and honey—called panchamrita. This liquid is later offered to the devotees. In the arghya, water is offered and the idol sips it in the achamana. The bathing of the deity is called snana and the dressing in silks and jewels is the vasana-bhushana. The welcome ceremony includes the offering of sandalwood paste, flowers, incense, camphor, and fire in the aarti lamp. The sacred food is called the naivedya and the achamana water is offered again for the deity to wash its mouth. All the while the priests recite the mantras as bells are rung and conches blown. Finally, the priest and the devotees prostrate themselves at the feet of the idol in the namaskriya to the royal deity.

Shiva, Vishnu, Rama, Krishna, Durga, Meenakshi, Mariamman, Guruvayurappan, Vitthala... the gods and goddesses have an amazing number of names but in the end they are all aspects of the one god, the supreme Brahman. Hinduism has this extraordinary capacity to absorb every kind of belief and let the worshippers pray in ways that give them the greatest satisfaction. A village woman may still lay flowers at the carved figure of a serpent goddess under a banyan tree. A more evolved mind may seek a formless, spiritually uniting one god. Another may sing to a romantic cowherd, a king or a wise saint. The Hindu pantheon of devis and devatas has place for all of them.

Tradition says that there are 330 million gods in the Hindu pantheon but the philosophers say they are finally the myriad personification of the great one god—the Brahman. Every worshipper imagines his deity in his own way and there can be as many aspects of the Brahman as there are devotees. So through the millennia Hindu mythology has become this intricately woven and at times highly confusing world of gods, goddesses, demons, heroes, saints, celestial dancers and musicians, sacred animals, trees, and rivers. And within this maze of deities there is always one that answers the call of every one who worships them.

CHAPTER TWO

The Gods of the Vedas

"Light us up with happiness, O Ushas, daughter of heaven,
With great lustre, O radiant one, with wealth,
O bountiful goddess.
Like a fair maiden comes Ushas, gladdening all
She comes awakening four footed beasts,
And makes the birds rise into the air.
O Ushas, shine with shimmering radiance,
O daughter of heaven, bringing us happiness
As you shower your light upon the daily sacrifices."

— hymn to Ushas, the goddess of dawn,
in the Rigveda

The word ved, means to know and the four Vedas are Books of Knowledge. They are a collection of hymns and ritual incantations that were sung during the ritual sacrifices, called yajnas. These hymns, called mantras, are songs praising the pantheon of gods of the early Aryans and in them we find descriptions of the great deities. It was believed that the Vedas were not written but divinely revealed and heard by the people. This was the concept of Shruti, hearing, and so for centuries these mantras were handed down as an oral tradition from one generation of the priesthood to the next. As much emphasis was laid on correct pronunciation, the text was memorised and recited with amazing precision and so the Vedas have come down to us relatively unchanged.

The Rigveda, composed before 1200 B.C.E contains 1028 hymns in praise of thirty-three gods and goddesses. The 10,589 verses, divided into ten mandalas, or cosmic sections, were composed over many centuries by many poets, often many generations of the same family of rishis, or seers. The Rigveda is at the heart of the Aryan system of religion while the other three Vedas are really extensions of this most important Veda.

The Samaveda is a collection of holy chants selected from the Rigveda for use during the sacrifices. As these sacrifices became more elaborate with complex rituals, a class of priests rose who specialised in the performance of the sacrifices. The third Veda, the Yajurveda has esoteric formulas, sacred invocations, the mantras and spells recited by the priests during the sacrifice. The fourth Veda, the Atharvaveda has a mix of hymns of praise and rituals, mantras and magic spells. Each Veda is divided into two sections—the Samhita with the hymns and mantras and the Brahmanas that are commentaries on the hymns.

The gods of the Rigveda are colourful deities. Magnificent kings like Indra and Varuna, auspicious like Agni and sacred like Soma. Among the goddesses are Ushas, Ratri and Prithivi. In appearance the gods and goddesses were imagined as ideal human beings and had a royal way of life. They rode through the air on horse-drawn chariots or on the back of animals and birds. The food they liked was the best food of the humans—oblations of milk and honey, grain and flesh. With it they drank the exhilarating juice of the soma plant.

Unlike humans, gods are immortal. The gods receive the prayers of humans and have the power to answer their prayers, by rewarding the good and punishing the evil. Some deities are somehow kinder than the others, others are more unpredictible and prone to anger. What makes them truly omnipotent is their ability to control the powers of nature, something that leaves us humans helpless. They can make storms cease and make the clouds rain, make the crops grow and if, angry, sweep the sky with thunder and lightning.

There was no clear hierarchy of the deities and every hymn calls the god it praises as the Supreme One. At times the same power is attributed to different gods. So both Indra and Varuna are called the king of the gods, Indra brings the rains and so does Varuna. The descriptions of the deities can at times be contradictory, changing from hymn to hymn. In one hymn Dyaus is the father of Indra, in another it is Tvashtri. The powers of Brahmanaspati, Prajapati, Brihaspati, and Brahma are interchangeable. Then many aspects of the same deity has different names and sometimes get treated as different gods. So Surya is also Pushan, Savitra, and Vishnu, Agni is Rudra, Varuna is Mitra. Still for a mythology that has survived for nearly five thousand years, the pantheon of Vedic gods is surprisingly vivid, well-ordered and fascinating in their colour and character. And among them if there was a trinity of powerful Vedic gods, it was the triad of Agni-Indra-Surya and with them was the celestial drink of Soma.

The gods also needed enemies they vanquished and evil they triumphed over. The Tattiriya Samhita puts evil in three categories—the asuras who oppose the gods, the rakshasas who are the enemies of men and the pisachas who trouble the dead. For the Aryans their enemies were the Dravidians and aborigine tribes that they were trying to conquer. So they were transformed into the demon asuras and rakshasas of their myths and shown being defeated by the Aryan gods. Primarily asuras and rakshasas were powerful kings and chieftains who were transformed into demons only because they opposed the Aryans. They acquired the bloody fangs and extra heads after this demonisation. The asura king Ravana, as we know was a scholar, worshipper of Shiva, and a successful king of a prosperous kingdom. His undoing was his opposition to the Rama Avatar.

The oldest commentator of the Rigveda, Yaska divides the Vedic gods into three sections according to the three divisions of the universe. So the gods can be celestial, atmospheric or terrestrial deities. The celestial or dyusthana deities are Dyaus, Varuna, Mitra, Surya, Savitra, Pushan, Vishnu, Aditi, the Adityas, Ushas, and the Ashvins. The important atmospheric or madhyamsthana deities are Indra, Rudra, the Maruts, and Vayu. The terrestrial or prithvisthana deities are Agni, Brihaspati, Soma, Prithvi, and Yama. If we judge the power of the god according to the number of hymns dedicated to them, then the three Indra-Agni-Soma were clearly the most popular ones. And most of them are benevolent deities with the exception of the volatile, malevolent Rudra.

CHAPTER THREE

The Celestial Gods

DYAUS–PRITHIVI. VARUNA–MITRA.
SURYA–SAVITRA–PUSHAN.
ADITI–ADITYAS. USHAS. ASHVINS.

> "O Light of the universe
> All shining, O great Surya
> Illumine everything with your light
> Spread everywhere in your vastness
> Your inexhaustible mighty radiance
> Resisting all the darkness."
>
> — Praise to Surya in the Rigveda

Dyaus and Prithivi

Dyaus is the oldest of the gods in the Rigveda whose origins can be traced back to a common Indo-European origin. Dyaus is very similar to the Greek god Zeus and the Roman god Jupiter, the remote personification of the sky and the father of the gods. In this paternal role Dyaus is often paired with the goddess of the earth, Prithivi. Together they are called Dyavaprithivi and are believed to be the universal parents. They are the first celestial couple and there is an ancient marriage vow that says, '*dyauraham prithvi tvam*'—I am Dyaus, the sky and you are Prithivi, the earth.

As the universal parents they lead to much speculation about who came first, Dyaus or Prithivi—she is the earth mother and he is the sky father. One hymn asks, 'Which of these two was the first and which the last? How have they been produced? Who knows?' The Satapatha Brahmana chooses the earth as the primeval source of creation and says firmly, 'This earth is the first created being'.

In the Vedas, Dyaus has no myths associated with him alone except a mention that he is the father of Ushas, the Goddess of Dawn. Prithivi, however, does generate more interest and there is an interesting myth about the earth goddess and a king called Prithu. During the reign of Prithu there was a terrible famine as the earth would not yield her fruits. King Prithu threatened to kill Prithivi if she did not yield and hearing of it the goddess took the form of a cow and hid in heaven. But a persistent Prithu pursued her and threatened her again. A terrified Earth asked how he could kill a female, at which Prithu replied that he would take on the sin of killing a female if it was of benefit to many. Finally, Prithivi yielded and said that she would help the crops grow with her milk but first Prithu would have to make the land level so that the milk can flow everywhere. Prithu did as she requested and the earth yielded crops again. This myth describes the beginning of agriculture when the land was levelled and then irrigated by the waters of the rivers.

Dyaus and Prithivi have six hymns dedicated to them in the Rigveda. In them Dyaus is described as a ruddy bull bellowing down from the sky, a poetic image of thunder and lightning and the arrival of the rains. Dyaus is also described as a black horse bedecked with pearls in a lyrical comparison to a starry night sky. Prithivi is the generous, giving earth and the Great Mother and with her are praised the many rivers like Saraswati, Vipasha (River Beas), Sindhu (River Indus), and Sutadri (River Sutlej) whose waters are described as the milk of the earth in the myth about Prithivi and King Prithu.

Dyaus and Prithivi are rather remote deities and there are few hymns in their praise in the Rigveda. Dyaus is always rather an abstract concept, who never crystallised into a rounded personality and is never praised alone, he is always spoken of with Prithivi and the goddess has just one small verse of three stanzas dedicated exclusively to her. Dyaus was already in decline by the time the Aryans arrived in India and was soon superseded by Indra, who was a much more active and creative god. Prithivi is still known but Dyaus has been completely forgotten, even his name has vanished completely from the mythology of today. Not only are there no temples to him, people no longer know of a great sky god called Dyaus.

Varuna–Mitra

In the beginning Varuna was the supreme king and judge of the pantheon, the mighty god who upheld the cosmic order. In the Rigveda he is called Samraj, the great king and Kshatram, the source of power. The warrior-ruler caste of Kshatriyas takes its name from Varuna's title and the rajasuya sacrifice performed by kings belongs to him. Initially he was superior to Indra, who would later supplant him as the celestial king.

Varuna's name is similar to the Greek word for the sky—Ouranos and he is among the most powerful among the celestial deities. The physical and moral order of the three worlds of heaven, earth and the netherworld is called rita and Varuna is the upholder of this rita. As he rewards those who obey the rules of rita and punishes the ones who sin, Varuna is both the moral and temporal authority and people were afraid of his powers.

Varuna, who is also invoked as Mitra, lives in a golden palace in the heaven and nothing misses his all seeing eyes. Mitra is never invoked alone but is always called with Varuna and they share their powers like divine partners. The waters are connected with Varuna and the plants with Mitra. It is Mitra who rules over the day as a solar deity and Varuna is described as the night sky and the stars are his spies who keep watch on the people on earth. Nothing misses Varuna's eyes, not even the thoughts in your mind. That is why he is also the lord of the spies. Later, the word 'mitra' came to mean a friend and Mitra presides over friendships. As creators of social and legal order, Mitra ratifies contracts and Varuna looks after oaths. Varuna is to be offered hot oblations and Mitra receives the cool offerings.

Varuna-Mitra is the all encompassing sky and his breath is the wind, the stars are his eyes and he shines with a 'sombre light'. Varuna establishes and obeys the rules because nature does so and it leads to peace and harmony in the universe. One hymn in the Rigveda says, "He follows the track of the birds which fly in the sky like the wake of a ship ploughing through the waves". So the hymns dedicated to Varuna in the Rigveda have an exalted, moral tone and are often prayers asking for forgiveness of this majestic king of the universe.

In some of these hymns he is called an asura who rules with the use of maya, the world of illusions and magic. Varuna-Mitra is a master of this 'asurasya maya' that keeps the sun in its allotted place in the sky. This can be confusing as later asura came to mean a demon but in the Rigvedic times it was the term for a lesser god and probably reflected Varuna's subsequent loss of prestige. Also, asura is similar to the Persian word for their god, Ahura, just as Mitra is connected to the Persian and later Greek god Mithras who was worshipped even in pre-Christian Rome.

Maya has also come to mean illusions and trickery but Varuna's maya is a beneficent magic that supports the movements of the heaven, earth, and air. It is this maya that makes the dawn appear, the moon to shine and the sun to travel across the sky. He brings rain and makes the river waters flow. Even though the rivers all flow into the ocean, the seas do not overflow because of the maya of Varuna-Mitra. In one song all the great rivers are described as flowing into the mouth of Varuna. One hymn in the Rigveda describes Varuna as the upholder of the laws of nature,

> "Wise are the races (of gods and men) through the greatness of him who propped apart the two wide worlds. He pressed forth the high, lofty vault of heaven and, likewise, the stars.
> And he spread out the earth beneath."

Varuna is the son of the mother goddess Aditi, and among his brothers is the sun god Surya. Later, Varuna was no longer the supreme power and became the leader of the Adityas, the sons of Aditi and by the time of the Puranas he had lost most of his influence. Varuna had replaced Dyaus and he was now eclipsed by the more martial Indra who was needed during the years when the Aryans were at war with the Dravidian settlers in northern India. Varuna was too remote and uninvolved. The Aryans needed a soma drinking, brawling, and aggressive god like Indra. What has remained is Varuna's connection to the rivers and the oceans and today he is remembered as the god of flowing waters, especially the oceans. He is prayed to by sailors and by farmers during droughts and he rules over the western quarters as a dikpala.

Varuna fell in love with the celestial nymph Urvashi and is the father of the sage Agastya. In the Ramayana, Agastya welcomed Rama into his ashram during Rama's years of exile. In the Vedic hymns Varuna is invoked mostly as the supreme judge and moral preceptor. He punishes with disease and death, so in every hymn there are passages asking for forgiveness for sins committed as the devotees fear being sent to the land of the dead called the House of Clay. One penitent prays,

> "Let me not go to the House of Clay, O Varuna!
> Forgive, O gracious Lord, forgive!
> Holy One, in want of wisdom I have opposed you.
> Forgive, O gracious Lord, forgive!
> Though in the midst of waters, thirst seizes
>   your worshipper
> Forgive, O gracious Lord, forgive!"

Varuna is dritavrata, the upholder of moral and ethical laws. He is described as a white man who rides this fantastic marine monster called makara with the head of a crocodile and the body of a fish. Varuna carries a noose, the pasha with which he binds sinners. He lives in Pushpagiri, the flower mountain in a golden palace with a thousand doors. He wears glittering star-spangled garments and sits with his consort Varuni on a throne made of diamonds. Varuni is the goddess of wine who appeared during the great churning of the oceans. The holy rivers, seas, lakes, water serpents, and the nagas all are in attendance in his court, as he is the lord of the oceans.

Varuna is Prachetas, the wise; Jalapati, the lord of the waters; Yadapati, the lord of aquatic animals; Amburaja, the king of the waters and Pasi, the noose carrier. Also he is Risadas, the destroyer of enemies; Tuvijata and Uruksaya, the mighty; Dharmapati, the lord of righteousness and Visvadarsata, the all seeing god. His image always depicts him as seated on a chariot drawn by seven swans. He is four armed, carrying a lotus, conch shell, noose, and a jewel box and he is served by the rivers Ganga and Yamuna.

In the Mahabharata, it was Varuna who gave the weapon, the Varunastra to Arjuna and he is also said to have saved the gods from Ravana. The Padma Purana tells the story of Ravana who was a scholar and a great worshipper of Shiva. After performing many arduous austerities Ravana gained a lingam from the god and he decided to carry this shivalinga from the Kailash mountain to his kingdom in Lanka. Through the worship of this shivalingam Ravana wanted to gain some of Shiva's power and then triumph over the gods.

The gods feared that if the lingam reached Lanka, Ravana would become too powerful. They knew that Shiva had made Ravana promise not to put down the lingam on the way to Lanka and Shiva had said that if Ravana lowered the lingam to the ground, it would not move any further. So Varuna entered Ravana's body and caused him such pain that Ravana found it hard to hold on to the lingam. Just then Indra in the guise of a Brahmin walked past and offered to hold the lingam. He then promptly dropped it to the ground and the lingam stayed there. In this way the gods were saved as Ravana could not establish Shiva's worship in Lanka.

Surya–Savitra–Pushan

For the people living in Vedic times one of the strongest presence in their lives was the golden ball that rose from the eastern horizon and brought with it both daylight and warmth, whose fierce rays dried up the earth in summer and turned warm and mellow in the winter chill. While the moon waxes and wanes, the sun is constant, an all seeing presence in the sky whose light is a source of life and healing. It was but natural that the sun would become a powerful god, like the god Ra of the Egyptians and Helios and Apollo of the Greeks.

Surya was by far one of the most majestic of the Vedic deities. No other deity has inspired such exquisite imagery and beautiful poetry as Surya. In the Rigveda, Surya has some of the most lyrical hymns dedicated to him,

> "Whose rays reach out to nourish the three worlds,
> Whom gods and demigods and men hymn together
>   as he rises,

Who fulfils the desires of his worshippers,
Homage to the Sun !"

Surya as the source of life in the world was worshipped
in many aspects, as the rising sun, the sun at its most powerful
and at sunset. He supports the sky during the day and enters
the fire at night to still provide the world with light. The god
gathered many names like Savitr, Pushan, Ravi and among
them was even an early appearance of Vishnu who would
become a god in his own right in the later Puranic period.
Some of Surya's aspects like Savitr and Pushan even gained
hymns addressed exclusively to them as solar deities.

Surya is the all-seeing god and is described as the eyes of
Varuna-Mitra during the day and like him he is an Aditya,
a son of the goddess Aditi. Surya is the greatest of the
Adityas as the giver of food, sight, health, knowledge, and
intelligence. He has been described as a ruddy bird and an
eagle that flies across the sky. At dawn, Surya comes riding
his seven horse chariot bringing light. He appears on the
eastern horizon and is driven across the sky by his charioteer
Aruna, an aspect of dawn. Surya is believed to be a healing
deity, especially for skin diseases. He is the source of the
Madhuvidya—the knowledge of honey therapy as an
antidote for poison. The famous Sun Temple at Konarak in
Orissa was visualised as a chariot of Surya. In a magnificent
show of architectural imagination it was built by the seashore
facing the east as if Surya's chariot had just risen at sunrise
from the foam-tipped waves of the Bay of Bengal. The
temple has seven stone horses in front symbolising the days
of the week and twelve wheels carved on the side for the

months in the year. The Sun Temple at Konarak is said to have been built by Samba, the son of Krishna, after he was healed by Surya. The story goes that Krishna became angry with his son because he thought that Samba had looked with desire at one of Krishna's young queens. He cursed Samba with leprosy but he realised he had made a mistake. Though Krishna deeply regretted his rash act it was too late, the curse had been uttered and it would come true.

A penitent Krishna asked Samba to pray to Surya for a cure. Samba had to search for the suryakshetra, the land of the sun, and worship Surya there. Samba travelled from Dwarka in the west, all across the land to Suryakshetra in the east at Konarak. Here as his malady worsened with time, Samba did not lose heart. He performed the severest of austerities for twelve long years and finally gained the blessings of Surya and was cured. In gratitude Samba built the first sun temple by the seashore at Konarak.

In the hymns in the Rigveda Surya is often addressed as Savitr, which means 'the stimulator' and scholars speculate that Savitr is the sun when it is shining the brightest, while it is addressed as Surya at sunrise and sunset. Sukumari Bhattacharji writes, "Savitra symbolises light, awakens life and impels men and creatures to action". While another aspect of the Sun called Martanda, symbolises the sun setting in the west. Martanda means the "dead egg" and the egglike ball of the sun was thought to die at dusk as it sank behind the western horizon.

The greatest hymn in the Rigveda is dedicated to the sun as Savitr. It is to the active, beneficent aspect of the sun that the Gayatri Mantra says "Tat Savitur varenium'—I worship thee Lord Savitr. This mantra is the holiest of all invocations in the Vedas and it has been the sacred morning prayer of Hindus for over two thousand years. No other mantra has gathered such immense meaning to it as this beautiful invocation to the sun, praising its golden splendour and asking for wisdom and enlightenment, "Bhargo devasya dhimahi. Dhiyo yo na prachodayat". The Gayatri Mantra is so resonant with sanctity that it has been called the mother of the Vedas and compared to the great trinity of Brahma-Vishnu-Shiva in its beneficent power.

Savitr is all golden, with a golden body, red-gold eyes, and a golden tongue. With his hair flowing around him like flames, he rides a golden chariot, like a deity created with molten sun rays. As he rides across the sky on his chariot drawn by white horses his arms reach out to infuse energy into all living things. He removes all evil dreams and vanquishes the demons. Savitr's name is derived from the Sanskrit 'su' which stands for 'to stimulate' and as he is a more active deity than Surya, he is asked to make the sun shine and bring light. Savitra is invoked both at sunrise and at sunset.

Pushan, another solar deity lacks the all-enveloping splendour of Surya and Savita. He has a beard and braided hair, he carries a golden spear, an awl, and a goad and rides a chariot drawn by goats. He is called the 'nourisher' and is a kind, generous god who brings good harvests. There is a wedding hymn dedicated to him where he is asked to take the bride by the hand and guide her to a new life. As he is constantly travelling across the sky, he knows all the roads and pathways. He is best known as a guardian of the roads and travellers praying for a safe journey sang to Pushan, the deliverer from danger. The gentle Pushan not only guides humans along the roads on earth but also accompanies them in their journey from life to death.

As his riding a goat-drawn chariot depicts, Pushan is a pastoral god, taking care of cattle and providing the beneficent powers of the sun for agriculture. Pushan is said to be toothless. The Mahabharata describing the great sacrifice of Daksha says that all the gods including the Adityas were invited, the only exception being Shiva-Rudra whom Daksha did not like. Furious at being excluded Shiva-Rudra kicked Pushan in the teeth and broke Savitr's arms. So during worship Pushan is offered a gruel made of ground rice called Karambhad.

When the Sun is worshipped, the dawn cannot be far away. Ushas is the goddess of dawn who at times is described as Surya's wife while in other hymns Surya is described as appearing from her. Surya also has a daughter called Suryaa and she is married to the twin Ashvins. In the Rigveda one lesser aspect of the sun god is called Vishnu. He is a minor deity here, a god who is responsible for the movement of the sun through the three worlds of heaven, air, and the earth. This is probably the beginning of the later Vishnu myth in which his Vamana avatar covered the three worlds in three giant steps.

Just as devout Hindus begin their morning by greeting the sun chanting the Gayatri Mantra, the yogi also performs the Surya Namaskar. Yoga being the philosophy and science by which to gain enlightenment also includes bodily exercises and the Surya Namaskar is the first of them. This yogic practice of saluting the sun is a combination of seven yogic asanas designed to greet the primal energy of the sun and harness its power to invigorate the body.

The Vishnu Purana tells us that Surya was married to Sanjana, the daughter of Viswakarma who is the divine architect. She bore him three children, Yama, his sister Yami or the river Yamuna, and Manu, the first human. However, Sanjana found his radiance unbearable and wanted to leave. So she got her twin sister Chhaya or shadow to take her place and withdrew into the forest disguised as a mare to meditate. For years Surya did not notice the absence of Sanjana until one day in a fit of anger Chhaya cursed Yama, one of Sanjana's sons and the curse took effect. Surya knew that no mother's curse against her offspring can take effect, so he confronted Chhaya and discovered the truth.

Through meditation Surya discovered where Sanjana was hiding and changed himself into a horse to subdue his light and went to live with her. Their union led to the birth of the twin Ashvins. While living in the forest in the form of a horse Surya communicated the Yajurveda to the seer Yajnavalkya. Surya and Sanjana finally asked her father Viswakarma for help. He put Surya's orb on his celestial lathe and cut away one-eighth of his brightness. With this bit of the sun Vishwakarma fashioned four weapons—the sudarshana chakra, Vishnu's discus; the trishula, the trident of Shiva; Shakti, the lance of Kartikeya, who leads the gods to war, and the weapons of Kubera, the god of wealth.

In the Brahma Purana there is a justly famous passage that describes with lyrical beauty the twelve forms of the Sun God, that encompass all his qualities. "The first form of the sun is Indra, lord of the gods and destroyer of their enemies; the second is Dhata, creator of all things; the third is Parjanaya, who dwells in the clouds and with his rays sends down water on the earth; the fourth is Tvashta, who lives in all corporal forms; the fifth is Pushan, who provides food for all living things; the sixth is Aryama, who brings sacrifices to fruition."

Then it continues, "The seventh derives his name from alms giving and rejoices all beggars by his gifts; the eighth is named Vivasvan and causes good digestion; the ninth is Vishnu who manifests himself to destroy the enemies of the gods; the tenth is Anshuman, who keeps all vital organs in good health; the eleventh is Varuna, who dwells in the heart of the waters and gives life to the universe; and the twelfth is Mitra who lives in the orb of the moon for the welfare of the three worlds. Such are the twelve splendours of the Sun, the supreme Spirit, who by their means plunges into the universe and irradiates even the secret souls of men."

Many Kshatriya clans, including that of Rama, trace their lineage to the sun and are called suryavanshi. One of the sons of Surya and Sanjana was Manu Vaivaswata, who is the first human. Manu Vaivaswata's son was Ikshvaku who was the founder of Rama's dynasty that ruled at Ayodhya. In the Ramayana, the monkey king Sugriva is a son of Surya.

The god plays a much more active part in the Mahabharata where Karna is the son of Kunti and Surya. It is Surya who gave the protective armour and earrings called kavach-kundala to Karna that made him invincible in battle. Just before the great battle at Kurukshetra, Arjuna prayed to his father Indra asking for help against Karna and Surya came to know of Indra's plans. So he came down to Earth to warn his son that Indra would come disguised as a Brahmin to ask for the armour as alms. He wanted Karna to refuse Indra's request. Karna who was legendary for his generosity would still give away his protective armour. Then during the great battle, when the vulnerable Karna faced the invincible Arjuna, like a true father Surya in the shape of the star spangled sky and the Ashvins came to stand behind Karna.

Another myth of Surya is about King Shatrajit of the Yadu clan who befriended the Sun God. Shatrajit complained that as the light blinded him all he could see was the radiance of Surya and not the real figure of the god. Surya then gathered all his brightness into a jewel called Syamantaka and gave it to Shatrajit and the friend could finally see the sun. Later, the descendants of the king fought each other for the possession of this jewel and nearly destroyed the Yadu clan.

This concept of the radiance of a solar deity being gathered into a jewel is repeated in the Puranic times where Vishnu has the Kaustubha gem that rose from the churning of the oceans. Another mythical jewel, the Suryakanta gem is said to be a crystal formed by the condensed rays of the sun. It is cool to the touch but still gives out the heat of the sunrays. Surya is also credited with writing a book—a celebrated treatise on astronomy called the *Surya Siddhanta* that is said to have been dictated by the sun. The poet Mayurabhatta, who was a contemporary of King Harshavardhan wrote *Suryasataka* in praise of the sun as the supreme god.

The iconography of Surya has always intrigued students of Indian art as in most of the sculptures he is depicted wearing a very un-Indian dress. Surya is shown wearing a long coat with a sash tied at the waist and high riding boots. It reflects the Persian origin of the horse-riding deity who would wear high boots. The cult of worshipping the sun is called Saura and traditionally the priests for the sun temples came from Persia and worship too was according to Persian rituals.

Surya is Dinkara, the maker of the day. As Vivaswat he is the radiant one. In astronomy, the planet sun is Ravi and as Bhaskara he is the creator of light. He is Arhapati, lord of the day, Grihapati, the lord of the constellations and as Karmasakshi, he witnesses the acts of people. He is Sahasrakirana, possessing a thousand rays and Martanda, the setting sun. In ancient times they worshipped Surya at temples in Konarak, Modhera, and Kashmir. The ruins of these temples still stand as testimony to the power of the life giving sun. Today, no more temples may be built to Surya but every day at sunrise his appearance is greeted with the chant of the Gayatri Mantra and the Surya Namaskar. As he watches us with benign golden eyes from the sky, it is hard to forget Surya-Savita, the supreme sun.

Aditi and the Adityas

Our ancient sages called her Aditi, 'Infinity' and 'Boundless'. In the Rigveda she is described as the mother of the gods. This mysterious goddess possesses all the undefinable qualities of the divine mother. Aditi is free and unbounded, like the endless span of the sky and like the changing face of the sky she has an elusive character and often contradictory qualities. In the Vedic pantheon she has a place of honour because her sons, called the Adityas, are some of the most important gods.

Originally the sky was the sole kingdom of Dyaus but as other gods appeared they took over different parts of the sky. From the sun and wind to rain and lightning, all these sky deities needed a mother. That was the divine Aditi and she gains importance mainly through the radiance of her powerful progeny. Scholars trying to capture her elusive, ever-changing nature call Aditi the personification of "universal, all-embracing Nature or Being."

The Adityas are "aditeh putrah", the sons of Aditi, and they are described as "inviolable, imperishable, eternal beings" and Aditi is the eternal element that sustains or is sustained by them. The Rigveda lists eight of her sons but by the time of the Satapatha Brahmanas and the Puranas the number had increased to twelve Adityas. Also, the names of the gods vary in different books and it is difficult to ascertain who were the original Adityas. Also as a god gained in prestige his worshippers called him an Aditya. Among them the notable ones are Varuna and Mitra who were kings of heaven, Aryaman, Bhaga, Daksha, Amsa, Dhatri, and also Savitr and Vivaswat, the sun gods. Later, even Indra is called an Aditya.

In the Rigveda, Varuna is the principal Aditya and so Aditi who is connected to life and sustenance, is also the upholder of the cosmic order of rita. Aditi is also intimately connected to light. The gods or devas are the lights of heaven who gather their radiance from a point in the sky in the east which is Aditi and it is from the east that two Adityas, the sun gods Savitr and Vivaswat appear. This is why none of the wind or storm gods are called Adityas in the Rigveda.

It is not easy to capture the essence of Aditi. In the Puranas Aditi is said to have married the sage Kashyapa and the Adityas are their children. To add to the confusion Aditi is at times described as the daughter of Daksha and at others as his mother. In the Yajurveda she is addressed as "Supporter of the sky, sustainer of the earth, sovereign of this world, wife of Vishnu". In the Mahabharata, Vishnu is called the son of Aditi in his dwarf incarnation and Devaki, the mother of Krishna, is represented as a manifestation of Aditi.

Some rather intriguing passages in the Rigveda mention that she went to heaven with her sons except one whom she abandoned on earth. It says, "Of the eight sons of Aditi who were born from her body, she approached the gods with seven and cast out Martanda". The Mahabharata says Martanda was born dead and Aditi did not take him to heaven because death belongs to the world and the Adityas are immortal. So he remained on earth to become Martanda Vivaswat, the god of the funeral ceremony of the shraddha. Martanda or the "dead egg" came to symbolise the setting sun and even received worship at the Martanda Temple in Kashmir.

Aditi is 'devamatri', the mother of the gods, is eternal and her resplendent sons are the radiant Adityas who reside in the sky. So she and her sons are the driving force of life on earth and she was worshipped for the sun shining in the sky, the rain brought by Indra and the justice of Varuna. As a free and boundless goddess they prayed to her for release from bondage of every kind. Aditi was invoked the most because she is a protective and forgiving goddess, the poet crying out to her,

"The august mother of the supporters of justice
   (Mitra and Varuna),
the wife of Order, we call you to our aid,
O powerful, ever young, far-spreading, kind
shelterer,
   good leader, Aditi !"

As she is the mother of Varuna, worshipping her provides
a way to reach that stern judge and king-god. As the divine
mother she is prayed to by people hoping for children and
by farmers to take care of their cattle.

Indra is shown as praying to Aditi saying, "Mother
goddess, do thou show favour unto me and grant me thy
blessings". According to the Matsya Purana, during the great
churning of the oceans a pair of earrings rose to the surface
and Indra gave them to Aditi, the mother he adored. Several
of the Puranas tell the story of these earrings being stolen
by Naraka, the asura king and taken to his city of Prag-
jyotisha. Krishna went in search of the earrings, fought and
defeated Naraka and brought them back.

Ushas

She is the beautiful maiden, all decked in pearls and silk who
shimmers across the eastern horizon to announce the arrival
of the sun. Ushas, the Vedic goddess of dawn is by far the
most beguiling goddess of the pantheon and her gentle, life
giving presence has inspired some of the most romantic
poetry in the Rigveda. She is invoked in twenty hymns,
sometimes alone and at others together with the Ashvins. For
the Vedic poet, she is this ever-seductive young goddess
coming to the world in myriad moods and colours,

With your graceful charms, for us,
O Dawn! Rise over us with your splendid light,
Heaven's daughter!
With light that makes the world look bright,
O Great Illumining Light!
You are the bestower of riches
O Goddess Dawn!

Ushas is one of the very few goddesses invoked in the Rigveda and she remains a beautiful phenomenon of nature and never grew into a multifaceted goddess. The descriptions are all around the natural beauty of the approaching dawn and the imagery is usually around an alluring woman. She is described as a dancer gaily attired in garments of golden light. The changing colours of dawn are like the swirling hues of the garments of a dancing girl. The gold tipped clouds are the jewellery she adorns herself with. She is ever-youthful because she is born again and again but she is also eternal and ancient. At times Surya is described as her lover but at others he appears from her. She is the sister of Ratri, the goddess of the night.

Ushas, the goddess of dawn, is the daughter of the heavens and the sister of the Adityas. The twin Ashvins ride across the sky escorting Ushas, as they together herald the arrival of the sun and then Surya appears, so Ushas and the Ashvins are friends. Ushas is always kind and generous to humans and animals, moving from house to house bringing light, health and wealth. And when she brings the gift of light, she does not discriminate between the rich and the poor.

Historian and linguist, Max Muller writing about Ushas says, "All this may be simply allegorical language. But the transition from Devi, 'the bright', to Devi, the goddess, is so easy; the daughter of the sky assumes so readily the same personality which is given to the sky Dyaus, her father, that we can only guess whether, in every passage, the poet is speaking of a bright apparition or of a bright goddess, of a natural vision or a visible deity."

Ushas is called Ahana and Dyotana, the illuminer and she rides across the sky on her bright chariot drawn by ruddy horses or at times cows. Her beauty has been compared to a pretty young girl, a bejewelled dancing girl, a young wife welcoming her husband and a langurous maiden appearing from her bath. As she dispels the darkness, she knows she is irresistible to everyone, waking all living things and making the birds fly out to welcome her. At times Agni, the god of fire, is said to be her lover and she lights the sacrificial fires.

This joyous and gentle goddess ultimately just remained the natural phenomenon of dawn and slowly lost to more intricately imagined and changeable goddesses. As the historian, Sukumari Bhattacharji comments about the eclipse of the dawn, "Ushas is too tangibly the physical phenomenon of the dawn to grow in dimension or to become a richer or more complex personality. Hence her personification is arrested early and post-Rigvedic literature forgets her altogether." Still the hymns that are sung to her remain some of the most lyrically unforgettable in the Rigveda.

The Ashvins

The celestial twins of the Ashvins are counted among the most important Vedic gods after Indra, Agni, and Soma. They are solar deities and their image is closely linked to the presence of the sun. The inseparable Ashvins ride out across the sky beside the dawn goddess to herald the appearance of Surya. Ushas is at times called their sister and at others their friend. They ride a golden chariot along a golden path and are known to be fond of honey; their chariot is called 'madhuvahana' as it is filled with it. Their whip scatters the early morning dew as they ride past. The Ashvins symbolise youth and beauty, light and speed, the power to heal and acts of generosity. And as their chariots appear across the sky before the sun,

> "Seers of great wisdom sing your praises
> As high above in heaven
> Your chariots soar like winged birds
> The Sun spreads its shining rays
> Its light licks around your chariots with a fiery tongue."

The Ashvins are the physicians of the gods, are kind and generous deities who brings health and offer miracle cures to people. In some hymns, Suryaa, the daughter of Savitra is said to be married to them. The physical basis of the Ashvins have puzzled scholars from the start and even Yaska, the first commentator on the Rigveda, was unsure which natural phenomenon the Ashvins represented. They could be the half light of dawn and dusk or even the morning and evening stars. Yaska says that their name derives from the root meaning "to fill" and so they pervade everything, one with light, the other with moisture. Writing in 'Nirukta' Yaska says, "Then who are these Ashvins? Heaven and earth, say some; the day and the night say others; the sun and the moon say yet others; but historians say that they are pious kings."

The Ashvins have fifty-four hymns dedicated to them. In the Puranas they are called Ashvinikumara, sons of a mare because according to one myth they were born to Sanjana and Vivaswat while they had taken the form of a stallion and a mare. They are handsome, young, agile, and swift and are the best riders among the gods. When Savitra wanted to find a husband for his daughter Suryaa, in the beginning he chose Soma but then all the gods wanted to marry her. The gods then had a horse race and the Ashvins won the tournament and the hand of Suryaa. In the epics they are the fathers of the Pandava twins Nakula and Sahadev who are known for their good looks.

The twins are called Dasra, bright, and Nasatya, the saviour, and it is their sunny healing powers that are praised the most in the prayers. The most famous myth is about their healing of the Rishi Chyavana. The Mahabharata and the Puranas tell the story of the sage Chyavana who was performing rigorous penance by the banks of the Narmada river. Over the years his body had become old and shrivelled. As he stayed still he was covered with an anthill with only his eyes visible. Sukanya, the young daughter of King Saryata while walking past saw the anthill and the eyes and out of curiosity poked them with a stick. Chyavana was furious and to save himself from the curses of the enraged rishi, King Saryata offered Sukanya in marriage to Chyavana. Just then the Ashvins who wandered the earth were going past the hermitage and they felt sorry for the young girl who had been tied to the decrepit old man. They offered themselves to Sukanya but the girl refused.

The Ashvins told her that as physicians of the gods they could restore the youth of her husband and she could then choose one of them. The Ashvins and Chyavana bathed in a pond and the rishi was a handsome young man once again. Sukanya took her time but then to his immense delight she chose him.

In gratitude to the Ashvins who had restored his youth, Chyavana decided to help them get an entry into the Soma sacrifices, which were the most important sacrifices in heaven. The twins had been excluded from these sacrifices as the gods did not approve of the Ashvins wandering among the people on earth and performing miracles. Indra was the most displeased and raised his thunderbolt to attack the Ashvins but Chyavana stopped his hand with a powerful curse and then created a huge demon that came rushing to devour the gods. Fearing for their lives the gods agreed to let the Ashvins join the sacrifice and partake of the divine Soma.

There is no iconography for the Ashvins and therefore no sculptures of these divine twins. By the time of the Puranas they were only invoked for their healing powers and remembered for their good looks. And in the epics every pair of brothers or friends—Nakula and Sahadev, Krishna and Balarama, Krishna and Arjuna are compared to the Ashvins for their handsome looks, kindness to people, and ability to ride chariots. The handsome healer-horsemen of the Rigveda never gained any temples for themselves.

CHAPTER FOUR

The Atmospheric Gods

INDRA. THE MARUTS. VAYU.

"Of Indra, I should first extol his mighty deeds
Which the bearer of the thunderbolt boldly performed
Slaying the serpent, he let flow the waters
Into the flooded streams and scattered the thick clouds."
— Praise of Indra in the Rigveda.

Indra

Indra was the most popular among the gods of the early
Aryans, who has the maximum number of hymns dedicated
to him in the Rigveda. Nearly a fourth of the hymns, two
hundred and fifty of them, sing the praises of this warrior
god, as he leads his army of gods with his divine weapons
of thunder and lightning. Indra and Varuna are both called
the king of the gods but where Varuna is a ruler, maintaining
the cosmic laws, Indra is the commander of the army leading
the gods to victory against demons.

When the Aryans began to move into the plains of north India they had to fight and conquer the indigenous tribal people. The pre-Aryan inhabitants of the land were called Dasyus and in the Aryan mythology they were often transformed into the demons being conquered by their gods. At this point in their history, much more than the law-giving Varuna or the remote Surya, the Aryans needed a swashbuckling fighter as the king of their heavens. Indra was the god who matched their needs. The Aryans sang to him and wove endless myths about his brave exploits. In many ways Indra is the most human of the Vedic gods. He is a mighty warrior, a bit of a brawler, impulsive, stubborn, who drinks deeply of the intoxicating drink of Soma before going out to battle. He is a fierce, merciless general who spares no one. He is often described as conquering a thousand cities fortified by stone walls.

Indra is the sun of Dyaus and Aditi and sometimes Agni is mentioned as his twin brother. He goes to war either riding his elephant Airavata or on a chariot like the Aryans who had ridden into India on horses. His horse is called Uchchaisravas, his chariot Vimana and Matali is his charioteer. Indra is heavily armed and his most powerful weapon is the Vajra, the thunderbolt. He also carries a hook, a bow, called the Sakradhanush, as it is made of the rainbow, and a sword, Paranja.

When going to battle the asuras, after drinking generous draughts of Soma, he rides out singing martial songs followed by the Maruts and the army of gods. Indra is all soldier and conquering king, as Sukumari Bhattacharji notes, "Morality, in the human sense, is not his strong point; he has bigger stakes to play for. Demons have to be slain, his people have to be provided with cattle, land, food and wealth; his country and kingdom have to be established. So he can hardly afford to concern himself with the niceties of conduct".

Indra's greatest feat was the defeat of his perennial enemy Vritra, the demon of drought. Hymn after hymn describes this epic battle that shook the sky.

> "The heroic deeds of Indra shall I proclaim
> The deeds that the thunder-wielder performed first
> He slew the dragon, freed the waters
> Slit the bowels of the hills.
> He slew the dragon resting on the hill.
> Tvashta had forged for him the shining thunder
> And the waters springing forth rushed towards
> the ocean.

Every year during the dry summer months, Vritra, who is a serpent, coils himself around the cloud mountains and holds the waters in the clouds, stopping them from raining on the earth. Indra, using his vajra and thunder, smashes Vritra's fortress of clouds and "frees the waters". Indra is also called Apsujit, the 'conquering in the waters' and this struggle has to be repeated every year. He also cuts a path for the rivers and with the release of the rains also come the happiness of a dawn bringing the sun and light. This image of a mighty god releasing the rains with thunder and tumult of noise resembles the advance of a victorious army. The imagery was used by the poet Kalidasa in his poem "Ritusamhara". Later, this role as the commander of the celestial army would be taken over by Kartikeya.

Indra is also a pastoral god and a favourite of herdsmen and farmers. The herdsmen ask him to protect their cattle, the farmers pray for rains with oblations of roasted barley cakes, meat, and Soma. Later, in the Puranic times this would lead to conflict between Indra and Krishna who was another pastoral deity and in the myth of the Govardhana mountain it is Krishna who would be victorious.

The mythic battle with Vritra began when a sage named Tvashtri created a son who had the power to defeat Indra. This son, named Visvarupa, had three heads. With one he read the Vedas, with the second he fed himself and with the third he saw everything around him. Visvarupa practised severe penances to gain the strength to defeat Indra. Feeling threatened Indra sent nymphs to seduce him but he was not moved. Indra struck him with his thunderbolt while the boy was at prayer and cut off his heads. To avenge his son Tvashtri created the monster called Vritra.

In the mighty battle that followed, Indra was defeated in the beginning and captured by Vritra. Indra called to the rishis for help. The rishis prayed to Vritra asking for a reconciliation. Vritra agreed on the condition that Indra would promise never to attack him with any weapon made of wood, stone or iron; nor with anything dry or wet. Also Indra had to promise that he would not attack during the day or night. With the help of his clever friend Vishnu, Indra found a way to circumvent these conditions. He attacked Vritra at dusk when it was neither day nor night, by a seashore using a weapon made out of a column of sea foam.

Indra is the god of the firmament, of the rains, thunder and lightning. He is described as a golden haired man with long powerful arms, and his chariot is pulled by tawny horses with flowing manes and tails. When not striking the enemy with his vajra or arrows, he uses the hook to entangle them in a net. He is described as destroying the 'stone built' cities of the asuras and the Dasyus. He can change his shape and fight in various animal and human forms. His character comes through surprisingly clearly in the hymns—of a fearless soldier who enjoys his food and drink, loves the company of pretty apsaras, and just as he is fierce in battle, he is generous to his friends. The hymns list innumerable asuras that he defeats and also mention the many weapons and captured horses, cows, and wealth that he gives to his devotees and friends.

The Vedic triad was of Agni-Surya-Indra and among the three Indra is the most active and approachable. He was also the favourite of the worshipper and there are many details of his life. As the gallant warrior-king he rules in heaven called Swarga with its capital named Amravati built on Mount Meru. With him is his queen Indrani whose hand he won after battling and killing her father. The exquisitely beautiful Indrani is also called Sachi and Aindri and they have two children, Jayanta and Jayanti. His palace is called Vaijayanta with gardens named Nandana, Kandsara or Parushya. In his luxurious court he is served by the Maruts and the Vasus and sits surrounded by beautiful apsaras like Rambha and Urvashi. It is easy to understand how the Rajput kings in the medieval period were often compared to Indra. He is the ideal image of the conquering Kshatriya warrior and king.

By the time of the Puranas, Indra had fallen from grace. By this time the Aryans were a settled race and felt little need for a warrior god. The later myths show Indra often losing battles to the asuras and even hiding from his enemies and asking for the help of other gods. Also, this is the period when the Brahmin priesthood was rising in influence and this very Kshatriya god is shown as angering the sages and being cursed by them like the choleric Durvasas, who deprived him of his favourite Soma.

Once Vishnu was a minor solar deity and Indra was the most important one. By the times of the Puranas it is Vishnu who is rising into prominence and many myths tell of the struggle between the two pastoral gods where Indra is vanquished. The most well-known is the episode in the Harivamsa where Krishna, the avatar of Vishnu, forbade the worship of Indra in Vrindavan. A furious Indra sent down torrents of rain over the land that could wash everything away. Krishna saves his people by raising the Govardhan mountain under which they take shelter from Indra's wrath.

In another myth, Krishna and his queen Satyabhama were visiting Swarga, Indra's heaven. Here Satyabhama saw the heavenly parijata tree and wanted to take it back with her. This tree had come up during the churning of the oceans and was the "delight of the nymphs of heaven, perfuming the world with its blossoms". Those who ate the fruit could remember their earlier births and if a woman wore these magical Parijata flowers in her hair she never lost the love of her husband. To please his wife Krishna carried off the tree but had to fight an angry Indra. Krishna defeated Indra and planted the tree in his capital Dwarka. After Krishna's death the Parijata tree returned to Swarga.

Indra also loses much of his martial powers by the time of the Puranas. Now his love of Soma has weakened him and he is often described as losing the battle against demons and seeking the help of Vishnu. In the Mahabharata is the story of Ahalya, who was the beautiful wife of the sage Gautama. Indra changed his appearance to look like Gautama and seduced Ahalya. When Gautama found this out he cursed Indra saying that his body would be marked forever with a thousand wounds shaped like eyes so that looking at him everyone would know of his crime. That is why he is called Sahasraksha, the thousand-eyed. Ahalya was cursed to wander the forests as an invisible spirit and she was saved when Rama came to the forest and forgave her. Here again an avatar of Vishnu is shown as being triumphant over Indra.

In the epic, Indra is the father of Arjuna and he plays an active role in his son's life. He gives him the weapon, Indrastra. Later, realising that the invincible Karna could defeat Arjuna, he disguises himself as a Brahmin and visits Karna while he is at his prayers. It was well-known that the generous Karna never turned away anyone and Indra asks for his magic armour and earrings as alms. These two things had made Karna invincible and even though he knew that the Brahmin was Indra, the great hero gave away his armour.

In the Ramayana, Indra's plight gets even worse. He is defeated by Ravana, the rakshasa king of Lanka who comes up to Indra's heaven to battle him. Indra is carried off to Lanka by Ravana's son Meghnad who earns the title of Indrajit, the conqueror of Indra. Finally, the gods have to negotiate with Ravana for Indra's release and, in exchange, Ravana gets the boon of immortality from Brahma.

With so many hymns dedicated to him, Indra also earned a large number of names. He is Mahendra, the great Indra; Sakra, the able one; and Swargapati, the lord of heaven. He is Vritrahan, the mighty destroyer of Vritra; Vajrapani, carrier of the thunderbolt; Meghavahana, borne upon the clouds and Devapati, ruler of the gods. He is Marutwan, the lord of the winds; Ugradhanwan, of the terrible bow and Purandara, the destroyer of cities.

The Maruts

Like a gathering of dark grey clouds and the fury of a gathering storm, the Maruts are the host of storm gods marching across the sky. They are minor deities but as gods of a natural phenomenon they are often invoked in the Rigveda. Numbering anywhere from twenty-one to three times sixty they bring storms, rain and lightning and are therefore the companions of Indra. When Indra moves across the sky with his vajra piercing the clouds, the Maruts are in his entourage. Like Indra they also drink Soma and move beside him, flashing across the sky, shaking the earth and the mountains before them. Some poems say the Maruts are the sons of Rudra, others call Vayu, the god of the winds, their father or credit Indra with their birth. The Maruts are brothers, born on the same day, and they always move together.

The Maruts are martial deities armed with lightning and thunderbolts and they "ride on the whirlwind and direct the storms". They are described as golden and ruddy, self-luminous deities who are partners of vidyut—lightning—and their chariots glitter with the silver glow of lightning. They are bejewelled gods, wearing helmets, mantles, armlets,

anklets, and garlands and as they move you can hear the roll
of thunder and the roaring of the winds. This is their celestial
song with which they inspire Indra as he rides out to fight
Vritra, the demon of drought. The rain that follows them is
like milk and honey falling from heaven. They are described
like soldiers going out to a battle, heavily armed with chisels,
knives, swords, bows, and arrows.

> "Spears rest upon your shoulders, O Maruts
> You have anklets on your feet,
> Golden jewellery gleam at your breasts
> Lustre in your ears, fiery lightnings in your hands
> And golden helmets placed on your heads."

The Ramayana speaks of the myth of the birth of the
Maruts. They are the sons of Kashyapa and Diti, the goddess
who is the antithesis of Aditi, the mother of Adityas. Diti
wanted a son with the strength and valour to defeat Indra.
Kashyapa promised such a son on condition that Diti bore
the child for a hundred years and lived an exemplary life.
Indra, feeling threatened, kept watch trying to find an
opportunity to destroy the unborn child. Then in the ninety-
ninth year one night Diti forgot to wash her feet before going
to bed, which broke the rule of ceremonial purity and taking
advantage of that Indra cut the embryo into seven parts.
Parvati, hearing the lamentations of Diti, asked Shiva to give
life to the seven parts and the seven Maruts were formed.

Their name is derived from "ma rodih", weep not, the
consolatory words said by Parvati to Diti as she wept over
her dead child. As Shiva granted them life, the Maruts are
called the sons of Rudra and in Puranic writing they are also

shown as companions of Shiva, wandering with him like mendicants, visiting cremation grounds. The names of the original Maruts are Vayuvega, wind speed; Vayubala, wind force; Vayuha, wind destroyer; Vayumandala, wind circle; Vayujvala, wind flame; Vayuretas, wind seed; and Vayuchakra, wind disc.

Vayu

Vayu is the god of the winds. He is also called Vata, the blowing breeze, Pavan, the purifier, Anila, breath, and Parjanya, a rain cloud. The Maruts and Vayu are at times interchangeable deities, both are worshipped for rain with Indra and also during thunderstorms to avert lightning. Vayu and Indra rule over the atmosphere but it is Indra who has the most Vedic hymns dedicated to him. The sage Atri's hymn to Parjanya in the Rigveda captures the tumult of the monsoons with exquisite imagery,

> "Like a charioteer lashing forward his horses
>   by the whip
> Does he announce the messengers of rain.
> Lion's roars from a distance are heard
> When Parjanya renders rainy the sky.
> Winds blow fast and lightnings flash,
> Plants shoot up and the heavens swell.
> Quickening showers fall for all,
> When Parjanya gladdens the earth with his seed."

Vayu is a martial, kinglike, handsome god who rides a chariot drawn by a pair of red or purple horses and like the roar of the wind, you can hear the coming of the chariot from far. When the chariot is pulled by hundreds of horses or more, their fury creates hurricanes and cyclones.

In the epic age, Vayu is said to be the father of many heroes in the Ramayana and Mahabharata. In the Ramayana, Vayu or Pavan is the father of Hanuman by a monkey mother. Hanuman is called "Pavan putra" and he inherited the power to fly from Vayu and possessed the strength of hurricanes. It was his swiftness and ability to fly that helped him to enter Lanka in search of Sita and later to fly from Lanka to Mount Kailash in search of the Sanjivani herb that saved Lakshman's life.

In the Mahabharata, Vayu is the father of the mighty Bhima, who is the strongest of the five Pandava brothers. There is also an amusing episode in the epic where the two sons of Vayu come into conflict when Bhima meets his brother Hanuman. While on his travels Bhima sees this old monkey with a long tail lying across his path and impatiently asks the monkey to move. The monkey says that he is willing to move but he is so old and tired, so would Bhima kindly shift his tail for him. Bhima, for all his legendary strength can't even lift Hanuman's tail and is amazed at losing a battle of strength to a mere monkey. The old monkey rises to embrace him as Hanuman reveals his real identity as Bhima's elder brother and the first Pavana Putra, son of the great god Vayu.

CHAPTER FIVE

The Terrestrial Gods

AGNI; SOMA; YAMA

"O Holy Fire, kindled bright with offerings
You protect man when he slips into a path of violence
Making him strong for the struggle of the righteous
O All-seeing Agni!"

— Praise of Agni in the Rigveda

Agni

Every ancient civilization has a fire god who is invoked and appeased. In the temples of ancient Greece, Rome, and Persia sacred fires were always kept lit and were worshipped with sacrifices. In the Vedic pantheon it was Agni who was the god of the fire, to be found both in the household hearth and the sacrificial altar. The worship of fire was central to the religion of Persia and Agni was brought to India as an important member of the Vedic gods. With Indra and Surya, he is a part of the Vedic triad of gods and even in later

Puranic times, Agni remained among the gods who were regularly worshipped, invoked every time the yajna fires were lit.

Agni is the priest of the gods and the god of the priests. Some priestly clans were worshippers of Agni and composed most of the hymns in his praise. Among them were the Bhrigus, the Kanvas and the Atharvans. Of these the Bhrigus were the most important and even their name means "born of flames". Sacrifice was the most sacred rite of the Vedic people and the presence of Agni as the medium of the yajna was central to it. It is Agni who sits beside the priest at the yajnas and he is called Hotri Varya, the chief priest. Over two hundred hymns in the Rigveda are dedicated to Agni,

> "All knowing as you are born at the altar
> For him who sets up the sacrifice of knowledge
> Bring all the gods who are awake at dawn.
> Served with oblations, O Agni of pious sacrifices,
> You are the messenger, the carrier of offerings
> And the charioteer to bring them here."

Agni appears in three phases, first he is celestial in the sky as the sun, then atmospheric in midair as lightning and then terrestrial as the fire on earth. So Agni can be found everywhere and he is a witness to everything. Agni plays a very important part in the ceremonies of the sacrifice and for all yajnas—from a wedding to a funeral—it is Agni who carries the offerings to the gods. He is the holy messenger because he is the mouth through which the gods eat the sacrifice. He wears a Brahmin's sacred thread across his shoulders because he officiates over the yajna like a priest. He is the mediator between humans and the gods and he is also the divine witness to the rituals of marriage.

Various gods are assigned different quarters, like Yama is the lord of the south, and they are called lokpalas. Agni is the guardian of the south-east quarter as one of the eight lokpalas and his region is called Purajyoti. He is a red-faced god with three legs and seven arms. He has dark eyes, a black neck, his hair flows around his head like flames, and he eats the oblations with his forked tongue shaped like flames. He is clothed in black and carries a rosary, a sacrificial spoon, and a flaming spear. His chariot is drawn by red horses, the seven winds are the wheels of his chariot. Vayu, the god of the winds, is his friend because it is Vayu who fans the flames. When he goes to war Agni burns his enemies to ashes. His food is wood and ghee and his face is smeared with melted butter because he drinks the melted butter of the sacrifice. He is also very fond of the divine drink Soma.

Agni is interchangeable with the sun and a source of warmth and light. He is born with the rising sun at dawn and then Surya, the sun god, enters the fire at night to still give light to the earth. So Surya of the sky, Agni of the earth and Indra of the air are brothers and they are the most important Adityas, whose parents are Dyaus and Aditi. However, unlike the other two, Agni belongs to the earth because he was left behind among people when the gods moved to live in heaven and as an Aditya he is the most important of the terrestrial deities. As the ram was often sacrificed at yajnas, Agni at times is shown riding a ram wearing the sacred thread and a garland of fruits.

The most fascinating imagery of Agni depicts him being born of two dead things, the two pieces of dry wood used to ignite a flame and he then eats the source of his life. So he has no mother to nourish him and has to be fed oblations of ghee to keep him alive. These two kindling sticks, the aranis, are at times called his parents, and as he is created anew with every fire, he is a handsome, ever young god. It is the fire in the kitchen that is at the heart of a household and this grahapatya fire is the most important one for daily life, used for cooking and for warmth. So he is referred to as grihapati, the householder and also atithi, the guest. As he sits at the the core of the yajna ceremony, he is called by many names describing him as a celestial priest. He is Ritvij, Vipra, Purohita, Advaryu and Brahman. He is the havya-vahana, the conveyor of the offerings.

There is also a darker side to Agni, he is like Rudra and Shiva, the lord of the cremation grounds in his role as the fire that burns on the funeral pyre. In this form he is Kravyad, the one who consumes flesh. The hell described in the epics is also filled with fire and in this terrible form Agni has two iron tusks and consumes everything before him. One famous hymn in the Rigveda is dedicated to this terrible aspect of the fire god, a prayer that even today touches the heart of the reader with its tragic cry,

> "Do not burn him, Agni, do not scorch him either,
> Do not tear asunder his skin or body;
> When you have devoured him, O Jatavedas,
> Then do you send him on to the Fathers.
> Let the eyes go to the sun, let the breath go to the wind;
> To heaven or to earth according to their desert."

In the Mahabharata, Agni appears as a god exhausted from devouring too many rich yajna sacrifices and he wishes to consume the Khandava forest to regain his strength. Indra opposes his plans but Agni succeeds in burning down the forest with the help of Krishna and Arjun who fight and defeat Indra. In the Ramayana, Agni helps Rama by becoming the father of Nila who is born of a monkey mother. Later it is Agni who bears witness to Sita's chastity after she is rescued from Lanka. In the Vishnu Purana he is called Abhimani and is said to be the eldest son of Brahma who is married to Swaha and they have three sons—Pavaka, Pavamana, and Suchi. During yajnas Agni's wife is also invoked when the worshipper calls "Om! Swaha!" while pouring the oblations into the fire. However, during offerings for the pitris, the ancestors, one invokes another of Agni's wives, Swadha.

In the Puranas, Agni is said to be the son of Angiras, the king of the pitris, the fathers of mankind. Among the Puranas, the one that is dedicated to Shiva is called the Agni Purana as it is said to have been dictated by Agni to the sage Vasistha. Another, the Vayu Purana, even tries to differentiate between forty-nine kinds of fire. Agni commands the riches of heaven and earth and he is invoked to gain wealth and for a long life and Agni, the fierce fire, receives prayers begging for forgiveness. Sometimes Brihaspati and Brahmanaspati, as celestial priests, are also called aspects of Agni.

The Brahmanas, which are the prose commentaries of the Vedas, give detailed instructions on the rituals of the sacred fire. These elaborate rituals of purification and worship can only be performed by a priest and there are three principal categories of sacrifice—the cooked food sacrifice to be offered at the family hearth, the oblation sacrifice, and the Soma sacrifice to be offered on the sacred fire, the homagni. Fire, water, and ghee are the essential ingredients of the yajna, as is the presence of the priest who knows the sacred words of the mantras.

The most important of the sacred fires are three in number. The one lit to the east is called the Ahavaniya or Vaisvanara fire to make offerings to the gods. The Dakshina fire is lit to the south and is for making offerings to one's ancestors. The west facing Garhapatya fire is the one in the homes for cooking and making daily offerings. The most elaborate is the full Soma ceremony that requires the presence of seventeen priests. The Agnistoma sacrifice is performed to conquer the kingdom of Yama, the god of death, and the Agnichayana sacrifice is for seeking wealth.

Agni has been given innumerable names, he is Vahni, he who receives the hom or burnt sacrifices; Anala, who burns; Pavaka, auspicious and Tomaradhara, holding a spear. Also Vaiswanara, son of the Sun; Abja-hasta, holding a lotus; Dhum-ketu, whose sign is smoke; and Hutabhuj, the devourer of offerings. He is Sukra, the bright; Rohitaswa, having red horses; Jatavedas, possessing the Vedas and Saptajivha, the seven-tongued.

Soma–Chandra

The most unusual of the Vedic deities is Soma. Instead of being a god it was the personification of a sacred plant and the drink made from it which had great exhilaratory powers. In later mythology, Soma represents the moon and also liquid coolness. Soma is both god and divine drink and as the god he is the Indian version of the European Bachhus or Dionysus.

Soma is amrita, the golden nectar and the precious ambrosia of the gods. It was deemed such a sacred drink that there are detailed descriptions in the Vedas of the way it was to be prepared. The shoot or stalk called amsu, was pounded between stones called adri and then the pressed juice filtered through sheep wool called pavamana. This extracted juice of the plant was made into a drink mixed with water and milk, sour milk or barley and drunk by the priest and worshippers during the yajna sacrifices.

Ancient Persia also had a similar sacred drink they called Haoma. The divine drink of the gods, Soma was quite clearly a very important deity with one hundred and fourteen hymns dedicated to him and as these hymns were recited during the yajna ceremonies, most of them were collected in one book, the ninth mandala of the Rigveda. Soma must have been a very popular deity as no other Vedic god has a whole book of hymns dedicated to him and in the verses the god and the drink are addressed interchangeably and also together.

The identity of the plant Soma has always intrigued scholars and there has been no definite conclusion. The mysterious Soma has been identified with many plants like hemp that is used to make the narcotic drink bhang, the milky climbing plant, Asclepias acida, and even a hallucinogenic mushroom, Amanita muscaria, commonly called fly agaric. It was probably not an alcoholic drink as there was no fermentation involved in the making of Soma. Also, it is different from wine which is called Sura. During the ceremony the roots of the plant were ground by stones, mixed with milk, and drunk immediateiy. The Soma sacrifice could be an elaborate ceremony using up to twenty-seven priests. From the verses that describe the effects of drinking Soma, it was probably an intoxicating drink that was also hallucinatory. Draughts of Soma made the drinker feel powerful and god-like, with vivid hallucinations of reaching up to the sky of an expanding universe.

As the Vedic people worshipped all phenomena that they could not explain, the drink also became a god next to natural elements like the sun and the sky. Soma made you feel immortal and they called it amrita, the draught of immortality. Soma also possesses curative powers, healing the sick and is a wise seer, a poet who stimulates thought and inspires hymns. One of the biggest drinkers of Soma was Indra who consumed it before going out to battle his perennial enemy, Vritra, the demon of drought. One of the most amusing hymns describes Indra's intoxication after some over indulgence with this potent drink,

> "The heavens above do not equal half of me.
> Have I been drinking Soma?
> In my glory I have passed beyond the sky
>   and the great earth.
> Have I been drinking Soma?
> I will pick up the earth and put it here
>   or put it there.
> Have I been drinking Soma?"

Like the Haoma of the Persian Avesta, Soma was first found in the heavens and brought to earth by a divine eagle and here it grew in the mountains. So Soma is the king of the plants, the lord of the woods, and is called Vanaspati. People prayed to Soma as a healer and also for immortality. One hymn pleads to him,

"Put me in the resplendent region where the sun
  is placed
And where there is no death or decay,
Where Vivasvat's son is king, where men enter the sun,
Where wide rivers flow, make me immortal there.
Where there is delight and satisfaction,
Where desires are satisfied, make me immortal there."

Later Soma became mystically linked with the moon as the moon is also identified as the god of the plant world but there is no clear explanation of this change in the character of Soma. By the time of the Puranas, Soma had become just another name of the moon god and the divine drink was no longer praised in hymns or taken during sacrifices. It is the moon who becomes Oshadhipati, the lord of medicinal herbs and the wise healer. Soma, the divine drink, is not mentioned in the Ramayana or Mahabharata though Chandra, the moon god, appears.

In the Puranas, Soma, as the moon, is said to be the son of the Rishi Atri and his wife Anasuya but he is also said to be the son of Brahma and to have appeared during the churning of the oceans. In the Vishnu Purana is the myth of Soma and the curse of Daksha. This seer had many daughters, one of them was Sati who married Shiva. Soma married twenty-seven of Daksha's daughters, who are personification of the twenty- seven stars like Ashvini and

Bharani and also the lunar month is of twenty-seven days. Soma gave more attention to Daksha's fourth daughter, Rohini, at which the other daughters complained to their father. Daksha tried to reason with his son-in-law and in spite of many requests from his wives, Soma did not change his ways. Daksha, who was known for his bad temper, cursed his son-in-law with consumption and the poor moon god began to turn pale. In a panic his wives rushed to their father asking for mercy but a curse cannot be taken back. So Daksha changed his curse so that periodically Soma could regain his health. This is the reason why Soma-Chandra, the moon god, waxes and wanes.

Another version of the same myth has Soma worshipping Shiva at Pattan by the sea in Gujarat and it is Shiva, moved to pity who restores his light. A grateful Soma built the first Somanath temple by the sea and the Shivalingam that he established in the garbhagriha is therefore called Somanath, or Someshwara, the lord of Soma. A temple legendary for its wealth stood here and was destroyed by Mahmud of Ghazni in the medieval times. Soma and Shiva are intimately connected in Indian mythology. Shiva lives in the mountains where the Soma plant grows, Shiva is fond of intoxicating drinks and both are connected to death and prayers for immortality. Both married daughters of Daksha and faced his wrath. It is the crescent moon that adorns Shiva's hair.

Another myth has Soma as an arrogant king who performed the Rajasuya yajna and carried off Tara, the wife of Brihaspati, and he refused to yield even when Brahma asked him to return Tara. In the battle that followed, Soma fought the gods with the support of demons. An angry Shiva cut his body in two with his trident and finally Brahma managed to convince Soma to return Tara. Later Tara gave birth to a son and reluctantly admitted that Soma was the father of the child. This child was named Budha, the wise, who is identified with the planet Mercury and became the father of the lunar race of Kshatriyas. The race of the Yadavas, who ruled Mathura, and the Purus of Hastinapur belonged to the lunar, Chandravanshi race. Krishna belonged to the Yadavas, the Kauravas and Pandavas were Purus. Budha is not to be confused with Gautama Buddha, the teacher and founder of Buddhism.

Soma, the moon, is described in the Puranas as a very handsome man riding a chariot of three wheels drawn by ten horses of the whiteness of jasmines. The drink is described both as white and also being tawny yellow. During sacrifices a red-brown calf was offered to Soma. The moon has many names. He is Chandra, Indu and Sashi, marked like a hare. He is Nisakara, creator of the night; Nakshatranatha, lord of the constellations and Sitamarichi, having cool rays. He is Sitansu, having white rays; Mriganka, marked like a deer and Shivashekhara, the crest of Shiva.

Dharma–Yama

In the Rigveda, Yama is the first man to die and so it was he who found a way to Pitriloka—the land of the fathers. In Vedic mythology, it is Yama's role as a god to gather the souls of the dead and guide them to this netherworld that he rules as god of the dead. In the Rigveda, he is treated as a minor deity, as Yama was first a mere mortal who gained immortality and only then became a god.

The early Aryans were an energetic, positive people very much like their favourite god Indra, and they were not too interested in creating a mythology around death. Yama is rather a benevolent god and the land of the fathers is a happy heaven where the souls are welcomed with all the delights and comforts they desired. In Yama's world, children once again meet their parents, friends are never parted, and husbands and wives are reunited. It is a paradise where they enjoy immortality with flowing Soma, milk, and honey. In the Rigveda, Yama only rules over this happy world and even though there is the concept of sin, there is no mention of the punishment of the sinful or of a hell.

Yama and his twin sister Yami were the children of Vivaswat, the sun, and Sanjana, also called Saranyu. They were the first mortals and the Rigveda has a hymn that is in the form of a dialogue between the two. Most of the mythologies of the world have a pair of divine twins who become the progenitors of the human race. Egyptian mythology had Osiris and Isis, the Persians had a similar sounding Yima and Yimeh, and the Greeks had Deukalion and Pyrrha. In this hymn, Yami entreats Yama to become her husband in order to perpetuate the human race but Yama rejects Yami's overtures as he says that those who preach virtue should set an example by practising it.

This hymn has baffled Vedic scholars who have speculated about its true meaning as it ends quite inconclusively. In later books, it is Prajapati who is credited with the creation of all living creatures on earth, not Yama and Yami. The historian Max Muller deduced that Vivaswat is the sky, Saranyu the dawn, Yama the day and Yami the night. So like day and night, they cannot unite though they are twins. The hymn also reflects a social condemnation of incest that had been accepted by earlier mythologies of creation. Yami was later transformed into the river Yamuna and came to be known only as Yama's sister and a minor river goddess.

In the Rigveda, Yama is a kind and benevolent god and does not have the role of the punisher of sinners. By the Puranic times, he had been transformed into Dharmaraja, the stern, impartial but merciless judge of the actions of human beings, their karma. By the time of the epics, Yama is no longer just a guide, but he is described as a god carrying a club who comes to collect the souls of the dead. After listening to their record of acts of good and evil he sends the virtuous to swarga, heaven, and the wicked to naraka, a burning hell. He is accompanied by two dogs named Syama and Sabala who have four eyes and wide nostrils. Like the Greek Cereberus, they guard the road to Yama's kingdom and the departed souls are advised to hurry past them. Similarly, Egyptian mythology has the jackal-headed Anubis who also guides souls to the netherworld.

In the epics, the writers were obviously fascinated by Yama and give detailed descriptions of Yama's netherworld. Yama's wives are named Hemamala, Sushila, and Vijaya. His kingdom, called Vaivasvataksaya, was built by Vishwakarma, the architect of the gods. Here in the city of Yamapura stands his glorious palace called Kalichi, where he sits on his throne of judgement called Vicharabhu. The door is guarded by his porter, Vaidhyata, his chief attendants are Mahachanda and Kalpurusha and the Yamadutas are his messengers who bring the souls before him.

Yama's chief clerk and councillor is Chitragupta who like St. Peter of the Christian heaven, keeps detailed records of the actions of mortals. Yama or Dharmaraja, is a fair and impartial judge and when a mortal faces him, Chitragupta reads out from his register called Agrasandhani, the good and evil acts are weighed on a scale and Yama passes judgement. He sends the soul either to the abode of the pitris, to one of twenty-one hells or back to earth to be born again.

Yama is described as a green man wearing red clothes. He carries a mace or club, a noose to capture the souls and is often shown riding a buffalo. He wears a crown and flowers in his hair. He is a dikpala and rules the southern quarters and so is called Dakshinapati. In the hymns, he is often invoked together with Agni, the god of fire, and they are described as sitting together at sacrifices. During yajnas, Yama is called from the southern quarters to come with the deified souls of the fathers to bless the performer of the sacrifice.

Indian mythology has no absolute evil like Satan who tempts humans to sin and rules over hell. The Indian belief is that each human being is the architect of his or her own fate, also that soul is indestructible and will never die. As the Bhagavad Gita says, the soul "is not slain, when the body is slain" and death is only an illusion. So Yama remains the ruler of the world of the ancestors and the judge and never plays an active part in the lives of mortals. Yama is invoked when the ancestors are worshipped during Pitripaksha, the fortnight of the waning moon just before Durga Puja in autumn.

In the Mahabharata, Dharma-Yama is the father of Yudhishthira. At the end of the epic, Dharma in the guise of a dog follows Yudhishthira on his last journey and tests him for his goodness and loyalty. The wise and incorruptible Vidura is an incarnate of Dharma. Even though he is born of a slave woman, he is a trusted adviser to the king Dhritarashtra and is the only one who protested at the injustice faced by the Pandavas. Krishna while visiting Hastinapur, chooses to accept his hospitality instead of staying with the prince, Duryodhana. As Vidura is Dharma, his soul merges into Yudhisthira after his death.

In the Mahabharata, the stern and relentless Yama meets his match in a young woman named Savitri. She fell in love with a handsome young man named Satyavan and married him despite knowing that he had only one year to live. Savitri spent the year in prayers and penances and on the last day of her husband's life she followed him to the forest where he went to cut wood.

In the forest Satyavan faints and dies and Yama appears to take his soul. But stubborn Savitri refuses to give up and follows Yama. Trying to get rid of the persistent woman, Yama promises her any boon except the life of her husband. First Savitri asks that her blind father-in-law should regain his sight. Then she asks for a hundred sons born of Satyavan who can carry on his name. As a boon cannot be taken back Yama finally gives in and restores Satyavan's life by releasing the cord that binds his soul.

Yama is invoked by many names. He is first Dharmaraja, the king of righteousness and justice after whom the treatise on law, the Dharmashastra, is named. He is Mrityu, death; Kala, time, and Antaka, the one who ends everything. Also Kritanta, the finisher; Samana, the settler and Samavarti, the impartial judge. He is Pitripati, the lord of the deified ancestors; Dandidhara, the one who carries the rod and Pasi, the one who bears the noose. He is Pretaraja, king of the ghosts; Shraddhadeva, god of the funeral ceremony; Samavurti, the impartial judge and Vaivaswata, the son of Vaivasta, the sun.

CHAPTER SIX

The Gods of the Puranas

I am the Brihat song of all songs in the Vedas.
I am the Gayatri of all measures in verse.
Of months, I am the first of the year,
And of the seasons, the season of flowers.
I am the cleverness in the gambler's dice.
I am the beauty of all things beautiful.
I am victory and the struggle for victory.
I am the goodness of those who are good.
                              — Krishna in the Bhagavad Gita

The religion that we know as Hinduism today, crystallised during the time of the epics and the Puranas. Hinduism's pantheon of gods and goddesses, its rituals of worship, festivals, myths and literature evolved to its present shape during the closing centuries before the Christian Era and the first few centuries of the next millennium. The mythology of the trinity of gods—Brahma, Vishnu, and Shiva and with them the Mother Goddess in her many forms is found within the two epics—the Ramayana and the Mahabharata—and the eighteen compendiums of miscellaneous writing called the Puranas.

This was the time when the nomadic Aryan tribes settled down in villages and towns along the river plains of North India and built temples to their gods. Also there was a growing interaction between the Aryan and the indigenous Dravidian population and a greater blending of the two cultures. Dravidian women entered Aryan households with their own gods and religious practices; neighbours joined in the celebration of festivals and priests shared their rituals of worship. This led to a change in the character of the Vedic gods and also the inclusion of ancient Dravidian deities and systems of worship into the Vedic religion.

Hinduism and its pantheon as we know it today had taken its final form by the time of the Guptas in the early centuries of the Christian Era. On their coins, the Gupta kings claimed to be the devotees of Vishnu or Shiva. They built temples where the images of the gods were consecrated and worshipped with rituals used till today. It was at this time that the worship of the trinity of deities of Brahma, Vishnu, Shiva, and Devi, the Mother Goddess, was developed into the form we are familiar with today. The Vedic religion consisted of communal worship through the performance of sacrifices to gods. It was now replaced by puja, a personal worship of an image in a sanctum and the gods who appealed most for such worship were the trinity and the Devi. For the common people, Indra and Varuna were remote sky gods who only listened to the priests. On the other hand, gentle Vishnu and an empathetic Shiva seemed to be willing to listen to the common people's small prayers. As the rituals of the Vedic religion were the exclusive preserve of priests, scholars call it Brahmanism and the latter form of personal devotion came to be termed as Hinduism.

During the epic-Puranic period, as the practices of Vedic religion gradually receded into the background and the Hindu trinity and Devi gained prominence, some like the sky god Dyaus and Soma were completely forgotten and mighty gods like Indra and Varuna became minor deities who were often defeated by Vishnu or Shiva. The abstract Vedic system of worship of sacrifices where the deity was an imagined presence was replaced by the puja of an image and the building of temples. So it was during the time of the Puranas that Hinduism finally got a pantheon and system of worship that gained universal acceptance.

What is intriguing is that the most important deities of Hinduism today were either minor gods or were unknown during Vedic times. There is no Shiva in the Vedas and only a minor god of similar qualities called Rudra. Vishnu as a solar deity was rarely invoked in the hymns and was considered just an aspect of Surya. As for the origins of the Devi, the patriarchal Vedic society had no important goddesses at all. It is hard to establish the precise reasons for the rise of the Puranic deities but somehow they answered a spiritual and ethical need among the people in a way the remote and detached nature gods of the Vedas could not. Vishnu and Shiva also gained power probably because these two adaptable deities have this amazing ability to absorb the qualities of other gods and cults and can appeal to a wide span of beliefs. As for the cult of the Devi in her many benign and malign forms, a matriarchal system of worship was just too powerful to be denied.

The epics and the Puranas, are the best source for the myths of Vishnu, Shiva, and Devi. By this time the enormous body of sacred literature of the Vedas, Brahmanas and the Upanishads was no longer accessible to common people as they had become the exclusive preserve of the priestly class of Brahmins. Not just the lower castes but even the Kshatriyas were not allowed to study them, as these holy books could only be studied by those who had undergone the initiation of the upanayana, the sacred thread ceremony. So the people created their own sacred literature through the epics, the Puranas, and a large collection of devotional hymns. They praised their favourite deities in poetry and song, created their myths and wrote their life stories. If the Hindu pantheon has survived virtually unchanged for a millennium it is because the trinity and the Devi are not the creations of an exclusive priesthood but of poets, balladeers, and mystics, voicing the thoughts and dreams of the devotees. They are the true deities of the people.

A new body of sacred literature grew which was available to everyone, from the Kshatriya king to the low caste weaver and even women. These were the two epics of the Ramayana and the Mahabharata, the eighteen Puranas, and an immense scholarly literature of commentaries and books on sacred law, philosophy, and theology. With it were the hymns that many mystic poets composed in praise of the deities and the most beautiful were the songs of the Nayanmars and Alvar saints of South India. The Nayanmars sang to Shiva, the Alvars praised Vishnu and their poetry has become the spiritual soul of Hindu worship. Popular Hinduism is based on these sources of thought much more than on the Vedas.

It is the southern part of India that gave Hindus this form of worship through bhakti, a mystical devotion to a god and the rituals of the puja. The greatest influence on the final form of Hinduism came from the Dravidian culture where ancient indigenous cults like the worship of a Mother Goddess had survived and with it there now grew a movement that propagated the loving devotion of a personal god. Beginning in the South, a fabulous literature of devotional poetry was produced all across the land and it went on right to the medieval period. These hymns became the foundation of the popular philosophy of Hinduism, where the devotee worshipped an idol of the deity by singing the hymns and performing the rituals of the puja. Though Brahma was counted among the holy trinity, it was Vishnu and Shiva who gained the most devotees and parallel to this ran the worship of the Devi in her many forms, at times as a consort of a god and at other times as a deity in her own right.

Vedic literature was not forgotten, it remained deeply sacred and the ancient system of sacrifices was still prevalent with yajnas performed by the priests but popular religion became a more personal form of worship. During a yajna a worshipper could reach the gods only through the priests as the ceremony with animal sacrifices and elaborate rituals was hard to understand. In contrast, the worship of an image with the more colourful rituals of the puja appealed directly to a devotee's aesthetic senses and a worshipper's personal involvement in the rituals gave greater spiritual satisfaction.

A devotee did not need a priest to speak to his god, he could perform puja himself, at home or at a temple. He had the Puranas which often provided details of the rituals, the hymns of the mystic poets to sing and the epics that told the stories of his god. The priests were now required for the worship at the temples and for elaborate ceremonies like weddings, funerals, and the yajnas of the rich. As the epics show, royal houses employed an army of priests to help the king perform the Rajasuya or the Ashvamedha yajnas. But Vishnu, Shiva or Durga also resided in a poor man's simple puja room and accepted the offerings directly from his hands.

Initially, the two great epics, the Ramayana and the Mahabharata, were purely secular literature. They were collections of martial poetry composed around the legendary heroes of the age, like Rama, the warrior prince of Ayodhya and Krishna, the statesman king of Mathura. These verses extolling their exploits are called itihasa, or historical epic poems and they were written by men, unlike the Vedas, which are considered sacred revealed literature, given directly by the gods. So in contrast to the Vedas which could not be changed or added to, the epics and the Puranas were the creations of many poets and bards over many centuries.

It is only gradually that some of the epic heroes were transformed into gods and other divine beings. Krishna was just a king and statesman in the Mahabharata, Rama was an exiled prince of Ayodhya, and neither were avatars of Vishnu. It is close to impossible to date the Mahabharata and Ramayana but they were written after the Vedas and earlier than the Puranas. The Puranas must have been produced later because they often contain excerpts from the epics. Also the heroes in the epics are mortal men but they had been transformed into deities by the time the Puranas were completed. The Vedas were composed between 1200 to 900 BC. The Ramayana between 200 BC to AD 200. The Mahabharata was begun around 400 BC but took its present shape only by about 300 AD and much of the Puranas were collated between the fourth and the twelfth century AD.

What makes the epics different from earlier religious literature is their origin. They were not written by the priestly class but by the class of traditional bards—a band of people's poets called Sutas. They travelled the land with their repertoire of martial and romantic ballads and as their livelihood depended on it, they made their stories as interesting as possible. They created a canvas of mighty heroes and the saga of their exploits became the basis of the epics. It is poetry composed more in praise of kings and warriors than gods and they talk more of wars and palace intrigue, not the rituals of yajnas and abstruse philosophy. But Indians have always liked to deify their heroes and it was not long before these heroes had gathered a large history of legends around them and been transformed into gods. Created by balladeers and poets, these gods became the personal deities of everyone regardless of their caste or social status.

What makes these epics so unique is that they are an amazing communal creation, composed over many centuries and added to by many poets who expanded the original tale. Initially the epics were a purely oral tradition, legends retold by the Sutas who carried their tales from place to place, stopping at temple precincts and village squares to narrate the stories of the valour of heroes, the perfidy of villains and the beauty of queens and princesses. These Sutas, were at times, charioteers who had witnessed famous battles and watched the acts of courage and cowardice, loyalty and treachery. So their combined experiences were incorporated into the tale until it became an intricate maze of myriad characters and many myths and legends. Sanjaya who narrates the Mahabharata was a Suta; Luv and Kush, the sons of Rama came to sing in his court in the guise of balladeers.

In the beginning the Mahabharata was probably just the history of a battle between two groups of cousins of the royal house of Hastinapur. But over the centuries, with every retelling, it gathered into itself the stories of other heroes and their battles, innumerable legends, myths about gods and goddesses and folk tales. Scholars feel that the Bhagavad Gita and the Harivamsa were added later and so were the first and last books of the Ramayana.

With the inclusion of the Bhagavad Gita and the Harivamsa one sees the transformation of Krishna into a god and it elevates the epic to sacred literature. In the Bhagavad Gita, Krishna propounds a philosophy that has become the basis of Hindu religious life and the Harivamsa narrates his life in mythical terms with miracles and magic. Similarly the Ramayana began as the story of Rama, the prince of Ayodhya who was banished from his kingdom and then went to war with the king of Lanka, Ravana who had abducted his wife Sita. Then two books were added to the original epic that transformed Rama into the ideal man and king and as an avatar of Vishnu into a god who is worshipped in temples.

The Puranas are simply called "ancient stories" and are a fascinating compendium of writing on various subjects ranging from religion, instructions on rituals, philosophy, astronomy, to praise of specific deities. Eighteen Puranas have survived and among them the most important are the Vishnu, Vayu, Agni, Bhavisya, and Bhagavad Puranas. They have been added to for so many centuries that it is extremely difficult to date them but they were probably compiled between the fourth and twelfth century AD. The sage Vyasa who is credited with the writing of the Mahabharata is also said to have collated the Puranas. Each Purana does mention various deities but concentrates on extolling the virtue of one god, either Brahma, Vishnu or Shiva. So the Vishnu and Bhagavad Puranas are dedicated to Vishnu and his incarnations while the Vayu and Agni sing the praises of Shiva as the supreme deity.

The Puranas also include the myths around local cults like the worship of snakes. The myths around snakes include snake deities like Vasuki, Takshak, Sheshnaag, and his sister Manasa. The elephant-headed deity Ganesha was probably worshipped in an elephant cult and was absorbed into the Shiva-Parvati sect as their son, just as Kartikeya may have been the god of a tribal peacock cult.

These Puranas are the greatest source for the myths and lifestories of the three main gods of Hinduism, the divine trinity of Brahma, Vishnu, and Shiva. They are written in simple, easy to understand verse and many of them have been translated into regional languages making them accessible to everyone and have thus not become the exclusive preserve of the priesthood. So it is the Puranas and their gods that are still known to people while the Vedic deities have lost their place in the popular imagination. If the myths about the Puranic gods are still so alive among people and their worship has such precisely elaborated rituals it is because of the easy accessibility of the Puranas.

The ideal Purana is supposed to have five sections called the Pancha-lakshana, the five identifying subjects. However, they diverge widely in content, with the Vishnu Purana coming closest to the perfect format. The Puranas are all written in verse, often in the form of dialogues between one character asking questions and another explaining. Quite often, the first enquirer is supposed to be a sage conversing with a god and the former then passes on the sacred words to his disciples. So Rishi Pulastya is said to have received the Vishnu Purana from Brahma; he then taught it to his disciple Parasara who expounded it to Maitreya.

Ideally the Puranas are supposed to cover five subjects. First, Sarga, the story of the creation of the universe. Second, Pratisarga, its destruction and recreation. Third is Vamsa, the genealogy of the gods and the pitripurushas, the deified ancestors. Fourth, Manvantra, the reigns of the primal ancestors called Manus and finally Vamsanucharita, the history of the kings of the solar and lunar races. The last topic often meant the genealogy of various royal dynasties were included in the Puranas and this has greatly helped modern historians in understanding the history of the period.

Some scholars feel the Puranas were also composed by Sutas as two of them—Lomaharshana and his son Ugrasravas—often appear as the narrators.The two epics and the Puranas are also different from the Vedas because they do not come down to us in a pristine state. They have all been added to over the centuries and there are many versions of each of them. This makes them great repositories of knowledge not just for the mythology and religion of the period but also its history and cultural life. Books like the Bhagavad Gita are the repository of the thoughts of great thinkers and have become the ethical anchor of Hindu life. The legends, fables, and parables in the Ramayana and Mahabharata have always enriched popular literature, inspiring not just books but also music, dance, and films. The Puranas are the foundation of the Hindu way of life, its rituals, festivals, ethics, superstitions and mythology.

Hindu mythology has always had this ability to change and transform itself to meet the spiritual needs of the people. As the historian Sukumari Bhattacharji writes, "Indian mythology was not a static affair, neither was it a luxury, it was linked with the vital spiritual urges and needs of the people, who projected their most haunting dreams, hopes and cravings into their myths." This is why Hindu mythology has not receded into books of ancient stories like the mythology of other countries but survived till today and Vishnu, Shiva, and the Devi are a living presence who still receive the worship of the people.

CHAPTER SEVEN

Brahma

*"When the gods made a sacrifice
With the Man as their victim
Spring was the melted butter
Summer was the fuel
And autumn was the oblation."*

— in praise of the Primeval Man, Rigveda

Brahma is the first of the omnipotent trinity of Hindu gods and appears as the great, cosmic creator. In the epic-Puranic times, the Vedic triad of Indra-Agni-Surya lost their pre-eminence to the all encompassing resonance of the magnificent trinity of Brahma-Vishnu-Shiva. And it is these three deities and the Mother Goddess Devi who are still the most popular gods worshipped today. Shiva, Vishnu, and the Devi have active cults and all the important temples are dedicated to them. In contrast there is no Brahma cult, no temples to him and in the popular mind his personality has remained a dim, shadowy presence, only evoked during sacrifices.

Hindus visualise existence as an endless cycle of creation, destruction, and creation again that starts with the beginning of time and will go on till eternity. It all begins when Brahma creates not just the earth and all its creatures but also the heavens and the gods and even the demons. Vishnu preserves this creation until its cycle comes to an end and then Shiva destroys it all so that creation can begin again. Among the three deities, Brahma somehow possesses the most amorphous personality. He replaced the remote and detached Dyaus, the sky father-god of the Vedic people but himself did not gain a strong identity.

Right from the time of the Rigveda, philosophers had been speculating about the beginnings of the universe. How did it all begin? Who was the first creator? How did this Supreme Being create? These are questions they began asking in Vedic times and we are asking even today. The imagination of the Vedic thinkers had spanned from a beginning in a great nothingness to a golden cosmic egg floating in the celestial waters and a primal god who created everything after his own birth. One of the most imaginative hymns in the Rigveda explores the mystery of creation in words that sound like the questions of a modern astronomer,

> There was no nonexistent; and no existent
>   at that time.
> There was neither the mid-space nor the
>   heaven beyond.
> What stirred? And in whose control?
> Was there water? The abyss was deep.
> Neither death nor deathlessness was there then.

> There was no sign of night or day.
> That One breathed without wind through
> its own power
> There was nothing other than this.

At this time many creator gods were envisaged like Brahmanaspati, Brihaspati and Prajapati. By the Puranic period it had crystallised into two deities whose character still causes some confusion in the minds of people. First there is the neuter Brahman who is described as "a sacred word, prayer, mantra, Omkara or a chant used as a spell". Then there is the masculine Brahma who is a part of the holy trinity and called the Great Creator.

Brahman is Absolute Reality while Atman is the individual soul. Brahman is the sacred syllable Om, the eternal soul which penetrates the whole universe and is its cause. So it is a highly abstract concept, he is the supreme soul of the universe and is simply called the One. Philosophers describe him as being . formless, the absolute deity who is self existent and eternal. All the gods merge into this great Brahman and the trinity are just aspects of this Supreme Being. Brahman is an obscure metaphysical concept that appeals to the philosopher but for people needing a personal deity he is hard to imagine and even harder to pray to. Brahman is always described in highly abstract terms as being the divine essence who is limitless, invisible, and uncreated. Sometimes reflecting this inherent obscurity he is addressed simply as Ka? or Who? The achievement of a knowledge of the Brahman has been the purpose of the meditation of the sages but this supreme being has never received the daily puja of the people.

The masculine Brahma is a much more active god as without him there would be no creation. The millenniums of earth years are like a blink in the eye of Brahma and his one year lasts for 2,160,000,000 years on earth. After his role as creator is over Brahma withdraws to sleep during this one gigantic Brahma year leaving the hard work of preservation to Vishnu. Everything decays and so does the universe that Brahma had created. So when the Brahma year comes to an end, Shiva apears as the Great Destroyer and everything is consumed by fire. Then Brahma wakes from his long sleep to create again and the eternal cycle continues. So he is a god who is present only for the creation and does not get involved in the mundane life of the people of the earth.

This detached, Olympian character made Brahma lose the worship of the people who preferred Vishnu and Shiva who are more empathetic gods. As a matter of fact by the time of the Puranas even Brahma's role of creation was being attributed to Vishnu. Today Brahma is only remembered as one of the trinity, there are no temples built to him and the only place where he is worshipped first is at Pushkar in Rajasthan. However, every temple to Vishnu and Shiva has a niche with the figure of Brahma and he does receive the worship of people as a part of the whole ritual of puja and he is always invoked during yajna ceremonies.

The creation myths are among the most complex in our ancient books. Instead of one, there are a multitude of stories with such a complicated maze of creators, cosmic fathers and sages who begin human dynasties that it is close to impossible to find a common thread among them. Surprisingly, the name Brahma is unknown in the Rigveda which mentions many creator gods like Brihaspati, Brahmanaspati, Prajapati, Tvastri, and Vishwakarma.

By the Puranic times Brahma had absorbed the role of these Vedic gods, who were all reduced to minor roles. Prajapati became the creator of all living things on earth, all plants especially medicinal herbs are created by him. Brahmanaspati became the god of prayers, who utters the mantras in which the gods dwell and he makes a yajna effective. Then he fades and is replaced by Brihaspati who is the divine priest, the purohita of the gods, who mediates between the gods and mortals and as he is the god of the priestly class of Brahmins he sits beside them during yajnas. Tvastri and Vishwakarma were combined and reduced to the role of the divine architect who planned Ravana's city of Lanka. Vishwakarma also designed weapons and chariots, like Rama's vimana ratha and Vishnu's Sudarshana Chakra.

The most interesting creation myth in the Vedas is of the golden egg. The hymns talk of all creation beginning with this celestial egg called Hiranyagarbha. The primal creator had appeared from the Hiryanagarbha who created the universe of gods and all living creatures from the broken shells of that giant egg. Scholars wonder if this golden egg is the sun. Every dawn as one watches this immense ball of fire appears over the horizon, it is easy to believe that this golden egg in the sky is the source of all life. As a matter of fact many of the world's mythologies from Egypt, Persia, and Indonesia also talk of a cosmic egg as the source of all creation. By Puranic times this primal creator who had appeared from the Hiryanagarbha was called Brahma. The Manu Samhita has a chapter on creation by Brahma,

SURYA
Vedic sun god whose golden rays are the source of light,
warmth and of creation.

INDRA
Vedic god of thunder and lightning.
The commander of the army of the gods.

KUVERA
Vedic god of wealth.
Half-brother of the demon king Ravana.

AGNI

The seven tongued god of fire
who is invoked during sacrifices.

BRAHMA
The god of creation.
First of the Puranic trinity of Brahma-Vishnu-Shiva.

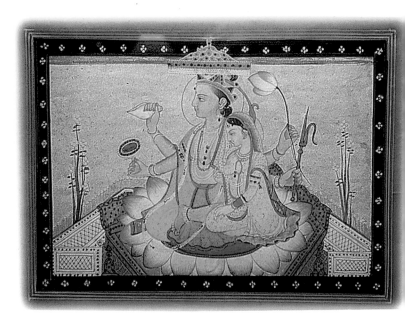

VISHNU AND LAKSHMI
Puranic god of preservation, second of the Puranic trinity
and his consort, the goddess of wealth.

BALAJI
The form of Lord Vishnu worshipped at Tirupati.
Also called Venkateshwara.

RAMA AND SITA
Warrior-prince of Ayodhya, seventh avatar of Vishnu,
hero of the Ramayana, Rama and his consort Sita.

"In this egg the blessed one remained a whole year, then of himself, by the effort of his thoughts, he divided the egg into two. From the two halves he made heaven and earth and between them the eight cardinal points and the eternal abode of the waters."

Brahma, being born of the golden Hiranyagarbha that was floating in the cosmic water, is a swayambhu, self-created and eternal and all his creations originate in his thoughts. Among them are the Rishis, the first humans and he also created Vak, the goddess of learning. According to the Ramayana, once he was born he took the shape of a boar to dive to the depths of the ocean and raised Prithvi, the earth goddess from the ocean bed and then filled it with living creatures. Later, as Brahma's powers waned, the boar who raised Prithvi, became the Varaha, one of the avatars of Vishnu.

Brahma is said to be the father of the seven Rishis, the Saptarshis, who are the first sages to whom the sacred hymns of the Vedas were revealed. There is also a constellation of stars named after the Saptarshi. Sometimes these Rishis are called Prajapatis and are said to be the fathers of the human race. Many of the Brahmin castes trace their origin to these Rishis. The Saptarshis are the mind-born sons of Brahma and the list of their names differ widely from book to book. The Satapatha Brahmana lists them as Gotama, Bharadwaja, Viswamitra, Jamadagni, Vasishtha, Kashyapa, and Atri. The Mahabharata lists them as Marichi, Atri, Angiras, Pulaha, Kratu, Pulastya, and Vasishtha. The Vishnu Purana adds Bhrigu and Daksha and increases the number to nine Rishis.

Another common world myth is of creation through a divine incest as the first god creates a female to begin the creation of the world. One myth says that the self-created Brahma, appearing from the golden egg then imagined Vak or Saraswati and with her, he began the process of procreation. So Saraswati who is the goddess of learning and speech and is the consort of Brahma is also called Manaskanya as she was created from his thoughts. This incest myth is unknown in the Rigveda and was attached to Brahma during the Puranic period when he was losing ground to Vishnu.

Another common world myth is of a celestial sacrifice that leads to creation. One manifestation of Brahma is of Purusha who is the oblation in a cosmic sacrifice. So if Brihaspati is the performer of the sacrifice, Purusha is the sacrifice itself. This transcendental god is "thousand-headed, thousand-eyed, who envelops the whole earth and is yet taller by a span." This myth is also the earliest description of the caste system as the four castes are described as originating from different parts of his body. "His mouth became the Brahmana, his arms, the Rajanya, his thighs the Vaisya and his feet the Sudra".

Brahma is described as being a fair skinned, potbellied figure, wearing white clothes and jewelled earrings. He has four heads facing the four directions, originally he had five but one was cut off by Shiva over a disagreement. So he is called Chaturanana, four-faced and ashta karna, eight-eared. His four hands hold the Vedas; a ladle used in sacrifices; a kamandal, the begging bowl of mendicants and a string of prayer beads. He is often depicted as an old man with a long beard and is at times addressed as pitamaha, grandfather. His vehicle is a swan and his heaven is named Brahmavrinda. As his consort, Saraswati is also called Brahmi and as Vak, the goddess of speech and learning who is said to have written the Vedas. Her vehicle is also a swan.

The Matsya Purana tells the story of how Brahma got his five heads. "Brahma formed from his own immaculate substance a female who is celebrated under the names Satarupa, Savitri, Saraswati, Gayatri and Brahmani. Beholding his daughter born from his body, Brahma became wounded with the arrows of love and exclaimed, 'How surpassingly lovely she is!' Satarupa turned to the right side from his gaze; but as Brahma wished to look at her, a second head issued from his body. As she passed to the left, and behind him, to avoid his amorous glances two other heads successively appeared. At length she sprang into the sky; and as Brahma was anxious to gaze after her there, a fifth head was immediately formed." Later this top most head was the casualty of Shiva's wrath.

As Brahma's power and popularity was gradually appropriated by Vishnu, his image also changed from a powerful creator to a god who is dependent on Vishnu and Shiva and is often defeated by them. By the Puranic times, the battle of supremacy of the gods is between Shiva and Vishnu, Brahma merely plays the role of the mediator. Shiva cut off the fifth head in anger after an argument that poor Brahma obviously lost. He is also described as worshipping Shiva. In the Mahabharata, Brahma is no longer self-created but instead is described as springing from a lotus that grows out of Vishnu's navel and Vishnu is depicted as both creator and preserver. This iconic image of Vishnu shows him in his eternal sleep of Anantasayana, lying on the coils of the serpent Sheshnaag and the snake's seven hoods are spread above him. From his navel grows the stalk of a lotus on which sits a much smaller figure of Brahma. More revealingly, if Brahma is called Purusha, Vishnu is Purushottam, the highest Purusha.

The temple at Pushkar has the most interesting myth on Brahma, related in the Skanda Purana. It is said that Brahma defeated a demon here and during the battle a lotus fell from his hand. Three lakes, the Jyeshtha, Madhyama, and Kanishtha pushkars sprang up where three petals fell and also gave the place its name, from pushp, flower and kar, hand. Brahma decided to hold a yajna at the site and asked Saraswati to attend. On the auspicious day, all the gods had gathered, the time for the yajna arrived but Saraswati had still not appeared. As a yajna could not begin without the presence of a consort Brahma asked Indra to get him a wife. He found a cowherd's daughter called Gayatri who was quickly married to Brahma. So when Saraswati finally arrived, the yajna had already begun and Brahma had a new wife sitting beside him.

A furious Saraswati stormed out of the yajna and pronounced the famous curse. She said that Brahma would be forgotten by the people and no one would worship him on earth. The gods begged her forgiveness and requested her to change her curse. A divine curse once given cannot be taken back but fortunately it can be modified. So Saraswati said that Brahma would continue to be worshipped only at Pushkar. The most important festival dedicated to Brahma is held at Pushkar on Kartik Purnima when people bathe in the lakes and do puja at the temples of Brahma, Saraswati, and Gayatri. Significantly, the two warring goddesses have their own temples at two ends of the town. The Pushkar festival also includes one of the largest cattle fairs in the world.

In the epics Brahma plays a smaller role compared to the omnipotent and at times warring Shiva and Vishnu. In the Ramayana, Brahma orders Valmiki to write the epics and he also appears personally at Dasaratha's sacrifice. He creates Kartikeya as the commander of the army of the gods. He presents the arrows for a bow that Rishi Agastya gives to Rama. Jambavat is his son by a monkey mother. He is described as cursing Kumbhakarna and also blessing Ravana with immortality. This blessing created a lot of problems for Rama who had to find a way to circumvent it. In the Mahabharata he is described as acting as Shiva's charioteer in Shiva's form as the Tripurantaka Murti, when Shiva destroys three asura cities and acting as his wedding priest in the Kalyanasundara Murti, when he marries Parvati.

Among the Puranas, the Brahma Purana is called the Adi Purana as it is considered to be the oldest. It was repeated by Brahma to the sage Marichi and is said to have contained ten thousand verses. The early chapters give a description of creation, however, the later ones have been appropriated by Vishnu and concentrate on the praise of Vishnu, especially of his avatar as Krishna and promote the worship of the deity of Jagannatha at the temple at Puri in Orissa.

Brahma is called Lokesha, the lord of the world; Sanat, the ancient and Pitamaha, grandfather. He is Shrashtri, the creator; Vidhatri, the sustainer and Adi Kavi, the first poet. He is Atmabhu, the self-existent; Paramesthi, the chief sacrificer and Hiranyagarbha, the one who appeared from the golden egg.

CHAPTER EIGHT

Vishnu

"In essence I am never born
I never alter.
I am the lord of all beings
And the full master of my own nature
Yet of my own power I come to be."
— Krishna in the Bhagavad Gita

Vishnu is a solar god and as the second god of the trinity, he plays the role of the great preserver. In Hinduism as we have it today, the worshippers of Vishnu and his ten avatars are by far the most popular sects, with temples in every village and town of the land. In the Hindu pantheon Vishnu is probably the most benign deity and deeply loved by the people because of his compassionate character. He is a benevolent, caring god who listens to your prayers, understands your dilemmas, forgives your sins, and offers salvation and mercy. His worship has a joyful, affectionate character with devotees swaying to songs and even dancing during puja and the offering of flowers, incense, and food.

As the sage Bhrigu wrote, "Here is the greatest of the gods. He surpasses others by the most powerful weapons, kindness and generosity." Vishnu is ever ready to intervene on behalf of righteousness and come to the assistance of those who ask for his help. Among the trinity Vishnu has the most human face and only a pure adoration is required from his devotees. As the Tamil poet Tirumalisai wrote around the 6th century AD.

> "When the grooves of the senses are barred and
>   sealed,
> When the highway of knowledge is lit with
>   wisdom's lamp,
> When intense pity melts the heart and eases
>   the bones,
> Then only can Vishnu, the weilder of the sacred
>   disc be seen."

Vishnu's rise to eminence is one of the most intriguing stories of the Hindu mythology. In the Rigveda, Vishnu is only one of the lesser aspects of the sun god Surya and only five hymns are dedicated to him. He is one of the Adityas and is merely the manifestation of solar energy. The only myth about him is a rather simple tale of Vishnu covering the seven regions of the universe in three giant steps. From this Vishnu would evolve into this many hued, complex god whose many manifestations needed ten incarnations, among them being the two most popular deities of Hinduism—the hero-gods, Rama, and Krishna.

The Rigvedic Vishnu represents the sun's disc and every manifestation of light—in the sun, in the fire, and in lightning.

He is the rising sun, the sun at high noon, and at the setting. At times he is described as a companion of Indra, moving in his entourage with the Maruts. The only connection to the later Vishnu is his being referred to as "the unconquerable preserver". By the time of the epics, he is not only the great preserver of every part of the universe including the sun but the Puranas even call him the creator, thus usurping the role of Brahma.

Vishnu's mythology is given in the greatest detail in the Vishnu, Vayu, and Bhagavad Puranas and the stories of his two most important avatars, Rama and Krishna, are given in the epics. The history of Ramachandra of Ayodhya is told in the Ramayana. The exploits of Krishna of Dwarka are found in the Mahabharata and in the Harivamsa, which is a supplement of the epic. The Mahabharata also contains the Bhagavad Gita which is by far the most important religious text in Hinduism and contains the teachings of Krishna about the correct path of life and the attainment of salvation. For millions of Hindus, the Bhagavad Gita is at the heart of their philosophy of life and a source of guidance, enlightenment and solace.

In the Puranas, especially the Vishnu Purana, Vishnu's character comes through most clearly. He is a divine monarch ever at work for the salvation of mankind, the perfect being who embodies all the satvagunas, the qualities of goodness and mercy that are the characteristics of the preserver. As this preserver he is called Narayana and is depicted as floating on the celestial waters of the Ananta ocean, lying on the coils of the serpent Shesha. Vishnu always has this quality of calm and repose, a compassionate detachment that contrasts widely with the volatile, unpredictible power of Shiva.

The most interesting element of the myths about Vishnu are his many incarnations called avatars. An avatar means a descent and it really stands for an incarnation, as a portion of the divine essence of Vishnu takes another form with super-human powers. One of the avatars of Vishnu is Krishna who in the discourse of the Bhagavad Gita explains the need for the avatars. Krishna explains that when the world is sunk in iniquities Vishnu appears in a living form to save the good and destroy evil. As Krishna says to the Pandava, Arjuna, in the Bhagavad Gita,

> "Whenever righteousness declines, O Bharata
> And unrighteousness holds sway;
> Then do I manifest myself in bodily form
> To protect the good, to destroy the evil
> To firmly establish dharma, the rule of righteousness
> I come into being from age to age."

The story of all his ten avatars from the man-lion Narasimha to Krishna have this common thread of good triumphing over evil with the intervention of a celestial aspect of Vishnu. As a warlike god Vishnu kills demons like Hiryanakasipu, Namichi, Kalanemi, Sumbha, and Nisumbha. This character of a champion of the good, as a compassionate god who listens to your prayers is what makes Vishnu and his avatars so popular among worshippers.

The worshippers of Vishnu are called Vaishnavas and among the greatest Vaishnava saints have been Chaitanya, Ramanuja, and the Alvar poets of the south like Nammalvar, Peyalvar, and the mystic poetess Andal. The Vaishnava sect gained popularity from the 4th century AD. and the first mention of the Bhakti of Vasudeva-Krishna can be found in the treatise *Ashtadhyayi* written by the philosopher Panini in the 5th century. The sect grew with the patronage of the Gupta kings. King Chandragupta Vikramaditya called himself a Parama Bhagavat, a worshipper of Vishnu and adopted the emblem of the Garuda Dhwaja—his flag had the image of Vishnu's vehicle, the mythical bird Garuda. The Gupta period is the time when temples to Vishnu began to be built and a definite iconography developed with images of Vishnu being carved at Mathura.

Vishnu and his consort Lakshmi or Sri, make a very attractive divine couple. She is the beautiful and gentle goddess of wealth and he is the wise preserver of life. Lakshmi's aura dazzles like lightning and from her body emanates the fragrance of lotuses. They live in his heaven called Vaikuntha and his vehicle is the mythical bird, the Garuda. The image of this half-human eagle is also placed on the god's ensign called the Garuda Dhwaja. In his icons Vishnu is depicted as a king, clad in silks and jewels often flanked by Lakshmi and Bhumi, the earth goddess. He is a very handsome god with a smiling benign face. He has a deep blue skin and wears golden yellow garments, a garland of lotuses, and much jewellery—bangles, earrings, necklaces, and a crown. On his breast he has a peculiar curl of hair called Srivatsa, he wears the Syamantaka jewel on his wrist and the Kaustubha gem on his chest.

Vishnu's image is called Sri Vigraha and it has four hands and carries the shankha-chakra-gada-padma—a conchshell, a discus, a mace, and a lotus flower. The conch shell is the

famous Panchajanya that he blows at the beginning of a
battle; the discus is variously called the Sudarshana Chakra
and Vajranabha, the mace is Kaumodaki, and the lotus is of
course the padma. He is depicted in three postures—
Sthanaka, that is standing, Asana, seated on a lotus with
Lakshmi beside him and Sayana, reclining on the coils of the
Sheshnaga floating on the Ananta ocean, with the serpent's
seven great hoods flaring out protectively over his head. In
the Sayana icon sometimes a lotus is shown growing out of
his navel with Brahma sitting on it.

Vishnu's iconography is one of most detailed with every
element getting names and some like the Sudarshana Chakra
even worshipped on their own. In spite of his benign
appearance, Vishnu is also quite a warrior and with his gada
he also has a bow, the Saranga, and a sword, the Nandaka.
His avatars Parashurama, Ramachandra, and Krishna are all
great warriors. Like Shiva has the lingam, the stone symbol
of Vishnu is the Salagram. These stones that have been
smoothened and rounded by the River Gandaki are
worshipped as a substitute for the image of Vishnu. His
favourite flower is the lotus and he likes the Tulsi plant, the
Vata or banyan and the Pipal trees. Some of the greatest
temples to Vishnu are at Srirangam, Kanchipuram, and
Alagarcoil in Tamil Nadu, Guruvayur in Kerala, Tirupati in
Andhra Pradesh and Badrinath in Uttaranchal.

Unlike Shiva who lives like an ascetic in the hills, Vishnu's
heaven is luxurious, deserving of a divine monarch. The
Mahabharata describes Vishnu's abode Vaikuntha as being
made entirely of gold, with pillars made of jewels. The
crystal-clear Ganga flows through it and there are five pools

with blue, red and white lotuses blooming in them. On a seat golden as the meridian sun, a resplendent Vishnu with Lakshmi on his right sit on white lotuses.

From the time of the Puranas, Vishnu has remained one of the most important gods of the Hindu pantheon. As scholars studying the rise of this god notice, his popularity comes from the ability to absorb the qualities of other deities, local cults, and even the legends of heroes. So he is a fusion of not just gods but also great kings and seers. First, he takes on the role of the creator from Brahma and eclipses Indra as a god-king. Then the legends of great kings like Ramachandra of Ayodhya and Krishna of Dwarka were incorporated into his mythology as they were included as avatars. Then great sages like Narayana were deified and became aspects of Vishnu.

What is interesting is that the concept of avatars is probably taken from the Buddhist belief in the birth of many Buddhas that can be found in the Jatakas and of the Tirthankars of the Jains. Even Gautama Buddha is included in the Vishnu pantheon as an avatar. The Buddha who began a heterodox sect that was critical of mainstream Hinduism was included as the ninth avatar in an attempt to raise the resonance of Vishnu. The myths of local cults like a cowherd god of the Abhiras of eastern India then became a part of the legend of Krishna. It is this many faceted, inclusive quality that has made Vishnu one of the most worshipped gods in the land.

While reading the myths in the Puranas what is fascinating is the underlying conflict between the worshippers of Vishnu and Shiva. The epic-Puranic times must have been a period of fierce conflict for supremacy between the two largest sects of the land as the thirteenth book of the Mahabharata is positively fraught with sectarian strife between Vaishnavas and Shaivites. Every Purana tries to prove the supremacy of one of them and there are innumerable myths that talk of one vanquishing the other. If Shiva triumphs by a show of his great power, Vishnu's successes come from a more subtle cleverness and a diplomatic demeanour. If the Skanda Purana tells the myth of the Jyotirlingam in which Shiva is shown to be supreme, the Bhagavad Purana tells of the myth of Bhrigu that shows Vishnu being worshipped as the greatest of the gods.

The Bhagavad Purana story begins with an argument among the sages about who is the supreme god—Brahma, Vishnu or Shiva. Rishi Bhrigu is then sent to heaven to test the trinity and discover who was the greatest. He first visits Brahma and entering Brahma's court he does not greet the god with the proper rituals of obeisance and a furious Brahma is about to curse him when Bhrigu saves himself by quickly apologising. He then travels to Mount Kailash and when Shiva comes to greet him with a welcoming embrace he turns away rudely. The volatile god promptly loses his temper and picks up his trident to kill him. Bhrigu is saved only because Parvati falls at her husband's feet and calms him down.

Finally Bhrigu arrives at Vaikuntha and finding Vishnu asleep he kicks him on the chest to wake him. Even on being woken up so rudely Vishnu springs up with a smile and welcomes the sage with kind words. He invites Bhrigu to sit down and then politely asks if he had hurt his foot and begins to massage it. A repentant Bhrigu is left speechless by such kindness and his eyes fill with tears of devotion and penitence. He hastens back to earth to tell the other rishis that it was Vishnu who was the greatest of the gods. Diplomatic and clever Vishnu is often shown triumphing by the use of quick wit and a sense of humour and this quality is most evident in his Krishna avatar. Krishna is considered to be a complete embodiment of all the qualities of the god.

Vishnu became one of the pre-eminent gods, eclipsing even Brahma mainly because of his avatars. Vishnu and his ten avatars within themselves encompass just about every quality that makes a god popular. Vishnu is seldom described as a vengeful or angry god. He is kind and compassionate, a god who has the patience to listen to your prayers but he is also willing to fight for the good and vanquish evil. Among his avatars, Krishna is a mischievous child, a divine lover and finally a majestic king. Rama is the ideal man and king and there are the ferocious Narasimha and the vengeful Parashuram to tackle the demons and cruel kings.

Usually the avatars are believed to be ten in number but the Bhagavat Purana lists up to twenty-two avatars and then states that in fact the incarnations of Vishnu cannot be counted as they are as innumerable as the rivulets flowing out of a lake. The first ten are of (1) Matsya, the fish; (2) Kurma, the tortoise; (3) Varaha, the boar; (4) Narasimha, the man-lion; (5) Vamana, the dwarf; (6) Parashuram, Rama with the axe; (7) Ramachandra, the king of Ayodhya and hero of the Ramayana; (8) Krishna, the king of Dwarka and hero of the Mahabharata; (9) Gautama Buddha, the founder of Buddhism, and (10) Kalki, the god who is yet to come.

The first five incarnations are purely mythological and not human and the original myths of Matsya, Kurma, Varaha, and Vamana were credited to Brahma-Prajapati in the Satapatha Brahmana. But the next four, of Parashurama, Ramchandra, Krishna, and Buddha show the deification of great kings, heroes, and an influential teacher. The most surprising is of course the transformation of the Buddha into an avatar but by the time of Mahayana Buddhism the Buddha was being considered a solar deity and it was easier to absorb him as an avatar. The ninth avatar is the most confusing of the ten, as some list Gautama Buddha and others mention Krishna's older brother Balarama. There are three Ramas mentioned as avatars—Rama Bhargava who is Parashuram, Rama Dasarathi the prince of Ayodhya and Rama Haladhara is Balarama who carries a plough as his weapon.

Every writer and poet of ancient times created their own list, praising gods, kings and sages they liked as avatars, including Purusha, the primal man, rishis like Kapila, Narada, Dattatreya, and Veda Vyasa and kings like Prithu and Rishabha. And even Yajna, the sacrifice itself, Nara-Narayana, two aspects of Krishna and Arjuna, and Dhanvantari, the physician of the gods, manage to get the status of avatars.

Shiva and Vishnu and his avatars were the inspiration for the greatest surge in devotional poetry in India. This stream of passionate devotion to a god is called Bhakti and it led to the composition of some of the most beautiful poetry from ancient to medieval times. From Nammalvar to Jaideva and Mirabai, this poetry has been at the heart of the Hindu worship or puja, where there is a personal communion with the god through rituals performed by the devotee and the singing of hymns. The songs of the Alvars who wrote in praise of Vishnu and the Nayanmars who worshipped Shiva are still sung in the temples of South India. The Ramcharitmanas of Tulsidas and the poems of Surdas and Mirabai have become a part of the spiritual heritage of the people.

Vishnu has a thousand names and the recitation of his Sahasranama is considered a very meritorious act of devotion. Among his names is Achyuta, the imperishable; Ananta, the endless and Chaturbhuja, the four armed. He is Hrishikesha, the lord of the senses; Janardhana, the one who men worship and Purushottama, the ideal and supreme spirit. He is the handsome and long-haired Kesava and the king-like Kiriti, wearing a crown.

As he floats on the celestial waters Vishnu is Narayana and because of the lotus that grows out of his navel, he is Padmanabha and his golden yellow garments make him Pitambara. He is Madhava, made of honey or a descendant of Madhu; Hari, the saviour and Mukunda, the deliverer. He is also Yajneswara, the lord of the sacrifice and at a yajna he is the priest, the oblation, the hymn, and the sacrifice itself. As Nara Narayan he is paired with a deified human like Rama-Lakshman, Krishna-Balarama, and Krishna-Arjuna.

The Ten Avatars of Vishnu

Matsya Avatar

In his first incarnation as the Matsya Avatar Vishnu comes to earth in the form of a fish. The first mention of a cosmic fish is found in the Satapatha Brahmana. In this early myth it is Brahma and not Vishnu who saves all creation from a deluge by taking the form of a fish. However, by the Puranic times the myth had been credited to Vishnu and the fish had become one of his avatars.

The Bhagavad Purana describes how Vishnu took the shape of a fish to save Manu Vaivaswata and all creation from being drowned during a great deluge when the oceans flooded the land. There are fourteen Manus who are the mythological progenitors of mankind. Each Manu rules the earth for one age of Manu called Manwantara that lasts for 4,320,000 human years. The first Manu called Swayambhuva was created by Brahma through the powers of his cosmic imagination and he is considered the author of the *Manu Samhita*, the first book that lays down the laws of mankind.

Vaivaswata, who meets the Matsya Avatar is the seventh Manu and he is called sun-born as he is the son of Vaivaswat, the sun god. Vaivaswat Manu is a Kshatriya and in some versions of the myth is also called Satyavrata, a pious and benevolent king. One day Satyavrata-Manu was praying by the banks of a river and performing the rituals. When he picked up a handful of river water, he found a small fish in the hollow of his hands. As Manu bent down to release the fish in the river the fish spoke to him saying, "You are a kind and benevolent king, how can you leave me in this huge river, at the mercy of its wild currents?"

Taking pity on the fish Manu carried it home and put it in a jar of water. Next morning he discovered to his amazement that it had grown so big that it could no longer fit inside the jar. So Manu transferred the fish into a small pond and pretty soon the fish had grown too big for it. As the fish kept growing Manu shifted it to a lake, a river and finally he carried it to the sea. Here, by the seashore, realising that this was no ordinary fish, Manu worshipped him. As the fish was about to swim away Manu could no longer contain his curiosity and asked the fish who he was and how it could grow so rapidly that a lake a hundred leagues in circumference could not hold him. "Surely you must be Bhagavat," concluded Manu, "The great Hari. But why did you come to seek my help?"

The fish explained that the world had become so full of evil that it was about to be drowned in a great deluge. He had come to save the righteous from this certain annihilation and Manu was among those he was going to save. The fish said that just before the great storm arrives he would send a ship to Manu who was to gather all the medicinal herbs and the seeds of all plants and trees, also collect pairs of all living creatures and then accompanied by the seven rishis he was to enter the ship and wait for the return of the fish.

Manu did what the Matsya Avatar had asked him to do and then sat meditating by the seashore. Slowly the winds began to rise, the skies became dark with threatening clouds that were split by thunder and lightning. Then the deluge came, an endless surge of rain and the sea began to rise with the waves beginning to engulf the land. Manu and his companions launched the ship on the turbulent waves and then they saw a gigantic fish with golden scales and a massive horn appear before them. Manu tied the ship to the horn of the fish using a serpent as a rope and the fish rode above the waves and pulled the ship to safety.

It was while the Matsya Avatar was swimming through the storm carrying the ship behind him that he dictated the words of the sacred Matsya Purana to Manu. Once the great storm had abated and all evil in mankind and demons had been drowned in its waves, creation started again with Manu, the living creatures, and the plants that he had saved. The myth of the Matsya Avatar greatly resembles the myth of Noah and the flood to be found in the Old Testament of the Bible, where Noah builds a ship to save all the living creatures from a great flood.

Another version of this myth found in the Bhagavat Purana adds a new twist to the tale. It says that during the time of Brahma's cosmic sleep a demon named Hayagriva had stolen the Vedas that were emanating from the mouth of the sleeping Brahma. So Vishnu came down to earth as a fish to search for him. During his stay on earth he saved the good Manu Satyavarta and all creation from the great deluge, then slew Hayagriva before returning the Vedas to Brahma.

Kurma Avatar

The Kurma Avatar has Vishnu appearing on earth in the form of a giant tortoise. Like the Matsya Avatar, the myth of this incarnation also first revolved around Brahma. In this incarnation Brahma is also called Kashyapa, which means tortoise. The Kurma Avatar is part of the myth of the great churning of the sea of milk that is among the most popular myths about the battle between the gods and the demons, the asuras.

It all began when Indra, the king of the gods, angered the sage Rishi Durvasas and the sage cursed him. To his consternation Indra discovered that he was losing his powers as a warrior. The asuras learning about the waning might of Indra, began to attack the army of the gods for whom defeat seemed imminent. As he was close to losing Swarga, his king- dom of heaven, a desperate Indra finally prayed to Vishnu for guidance.

Vishnu said that the only solution was for Indra to find the pot of amrita, the nectar of immortality which would make the gods invincible in battle. This divine ambrosia had been lost during the great deluge and now lay at the bottom of the sea of milk and the sea would have to be churned to recover it.

"This is what you must do," said Vishnu,"take Mount Mandara as a stick and the snake Vasuki as a rope and churn the sea of milk, and you will see it produce the liquid of immortality and other wonderful presents. But you must have the help of the demons. Make an alliance with them and tell them that you will share with them the fruits of your common labour. I shall myself take care that they don't get their share of the ambrosia."

So the gods promised a share of the amrita to the asuras and then using the snake Vasuki as the rope and Mandara as the stick they began the mighty churning of the sea of milk. The movement was so violent that the slopes of the mountain became red hot and all the creatures living there were close to dying. So Indra sent a shower of rain to cool the mountain and saved the creatures. As the asuras and gods pulled and twisted, the heavy Mandara threatened to break through the surface of the earth itself and again the gods prayed to Vishnu for help. Vishnu then took the form of a giant tortoise and placed himself below the mountain as a pivot so that the churning could continue.

During the churning Vishnu was everywhere. He was the pivot, he sat resplendent on the peak of the mountain and he was also present among the gods and asuras pulling the rope. Poor Vasuki suffered greatly from all the pulling. The gods were holding his tail and the asuras had his head. His venom began to pour out of his mouth in a stream that threatened to destroy all animals, birds, and trees on earth and even the demons and the gods. In great distress they all called out to Shiva to save them and even Vishnu joined their prayers. Shiva saved all creation by drinking this poison that burnt his neck and turned it a dark blue that earned him the name of Nilkantha.

Finally the hard work began to bear fruit and mystical and magical things began to rise to the surface. First appeared Surabhi, the cow of plenty; then Varuni, the goddess of wine and Parijata, the marvellous tree of paradise whose flowers filled the heavens with heady fragrance. Then appeared Chandra, the moon god that Shiva picked up and placed on his head. Next to appear was Lakshmi, the goddess of wealth, sitting beautiful and radiant on a white lotus, wearing a crown of ever fresh flowers. At her appearance the gandharvas, the heavenly musicians, began to play, the rishis sang her praises and the sacred elephants poured the waters of the Ganga over her from golden ewers. Lakshmi, as Vishnu's consort went and sat on his knee and refused to look at the asuras who were also keen to possess her.

Among the other celestial things to rise with the churning was the most graceful of the nymphs, the apsara Rambha; Uchhaisravas, a wonderful horse; Kaustubha, the magical jewel that Vishnu wears; Airavat the great elephant of Indra;

Shankha the magical conch shell of victory and Dhanus, the powerful bow.

Finally Dhanvantari, the physician of the gods and the inventor of the ayurveda system of medicine, rose to the surface carrying the pot of amrita. Battle commenced immediately between the gods and the demons for this nectar of life and the asuras managed to take it away. Then Vishnu appeared before them as a beautiful woman and as the asuras were arguing among themselves about who should possess her, he sneaked away with the amrita.

Vishnu flew away on the back of Garuda, carrying this kumbha of amrita. On his journey from the sea of milk to Swarga he flew above the land and a few drops of the amrita fell on earth. The four places where the amrita fell are at Allahabad in Uttar Pradesh, Haridwar in Uttaranchal, Ujjain in Madhya Pradesh and Nasik in Maharashtra and here the great congregation of the Kumbh Melas are held. As the journey took twelve human years, the Maha Kumbh is held every twelve years at Allahabad. This Mahakumbh is considered the most sacred, with crores of people bathing at the confluence of the three rivers—the Ganga, the Yamuna, and the mysterious, invisible Saraswati. The tradition of the Kumbh Mela goes back centuries and was probably begun by the Adi Shankaracharya in the 8th century and it still celebrates Vishnu's appearance as a tortoise in the Kurma Avatar.

Varaha Avatar

The Varaha Avatar is Vishnu's incarnation as a boar. Unlike the Matsya and Kurma avatars that were not worshipped except as a part of all the ten avatars, the Varaha Avatar was once a popular deity. During the Gupta period there were temples dedicated to this avatar and there are many depictions of him in sculptures and paintings.

The first mention of a god taking the form of a giant boar can be found in the Taittriya Samhita where it is said that Prithivi, the earth goddess, had sunk to the bottom of the ocean and all creation was threatened with destruction. So Brahma took the form of a boar, dived down to the sea bed and raised Prithivi to the surface, carrying her on his tusk.

By the time the myth of the Varaha Avatar was being told in the Puranas, the boar had been transformed into an avatar of Vishnu and a simple tale of the rescue of the earth goddess now had another tale of Vishnu battling a demon woven into it. This demon named Hiranyaksha had been introduced because in all his incarnations Vishnu had to come to earth to save the good and punish the evil.

In his earlier birth Hiranyaksha had been the doorkeeper in Vishnu's palace. Once when some rishis came to see Vishnu, he was rude to them and the sages cursed him that he would be born as an asura son of Diti. In his next birth as the demon Hiranyaksha he hated Vishnu. During the deluge when the earth had been flooded by water Hiranyaksha kidnapped the beautiful Prithivi, the earth goddess and dragging her to the bottom of the ocean, he held her captive there.

Vishnu then took the form of the Varaha Avatar and the Vayu Purana describes this magnificent creature. "The boar was ten yojanas in breadth and a thousand yojanas in height; his colour was like a dark cloud and his roar like thunder. His bulk was vast as a mountain; his tusks were white, sharp and fearful; fire flashed from his eyes like lightning and he was radiant as the sun. His shoulders were round, fat and large and he strode along like a powerful lion."

The Varaha Avatar tracked Prithivi by his sense of smell and he plunged into the ocean to save her. Here Hiranyaksha was waiting for him and a terrific battle began that lasted for a thousand years until finally the Varaha Avatar managed to vanquish and kill the asura. Then Vishnu picked up Prithivi and placed her on his tusk and rose to the surface. This triumph over Hiryanyaksha would lead to Vishnu coming down to earth in his next avatar as Narasimha, the man-lion, to fight Hiranyakasipu, who was the brother of the asura he had killed.

The Varaha Avatar and its powerful myth was not just worshipped—it also inspired many magnificent sculptures that depict this giant human figure with the head of a boar carrying the tiny female figure of the fragile Prithivi on his tusk or on one protective arm. On the walls of the caves of Udaigiri in Madhya Pradesh in a composition of great power and beauty, the carving of the Varaha Avatar is surrounded by an admiring throng of gods and goddesses, flying nymphs, and bearded sages praying to him.

Narasimha Avatar

The fourth incarnation of Vishnu is as the Narasimha Avatar, a ferocious half-man, half- lion creature. The first four avatars of Matsya, Kurma, Varaha, and Narasimha are all purely mythological creatures and they are all supposed to have appeared in the Satya Yuga. As the cycle of creation is divided into four Yugas, the first is the Satya Yuga. One complete cycle of four Yugas is of four million human years but is just one year in the life of Brahma.

The asura king Hiryanyakasipu was the brother of the demon Hiranyaksha who had been slain by the Varaha Avatar of Vishnu. Hiranyakasipu prayed to Brahma and performed severe penances for many years and when finally Brahma offered to grant him a boon he asked to be made immortal. Brahma laughed and said that as he himself was not immortal he did not have the power to grant such a blessing. So Hiranyakasipu begged to be made invincible in battle. His boon had to be that he could not be killed by any man or animal or by any weapon. He could not be defeated by day or night; in the air, earth or water and neither inside nor outside a house. A reluctant Brahma had to grant this benediction.

A triumphant Hiranyakasipu went to war against the gods, who were helpless before his might and pretty soon he was the ruler of the three worlds. He disliked all the gods but if there was any deity he truly hated it was Vishnu who had killed his brother Hiranyaksha. So his utter horror can be imagined when he discovered that his young son Prahlada had become a fervent devotee of Vishnu. The demon king tried hard to convince the boy of his mistake but Prahlada was firm in his faith. As time went by his fervour grew and he went about singing the praises of Vishnu to everyone.

Then as Prahlada even tried to convert his father to the worship of Vishnu, the angry demon finally decided that he had to kill his son. Many attempts were made to slay Prahlada but they all failed. The wild elephants that were sent to trample him, lay down at his feet like docile pets. He was given poison and the boy drank it like a honeyed drink. He was thrown into the ocean and the angry ocean threatened to flood the land if he wasn't rescued. The fires could not touch him, when he was thrown off a mountain, Prithivi, the earth goddess, received him gently in her lap.

An enraged Hiranyakasipu ordered Prahlada not to praise Vishnu and the boy replied, "I cannot obey you father. Wherever I look, all I see is Vishnu."

"If Vishnu is everywhere," said Hiranyakasipu, "how is it I cannot see him?" Then he pointed to a pillar and asked, "Is your Vishnu there?" As Prahlada nodded, he kicked the pillar shouting curses at Vishnu.

The pillar crashed to the ground and broke and from it a giant figure of a man with a lion's head appeared. This was the Narasimha Avatar of Vishnu and he picked up Hiranyakasipu, laid him across his lap and using his long nails he tore the demon's body to shreds.

The Narasimha Avatar succeeded in killing Hiranyakasipu in spite of Brahma's boon of invincibility. As a man-lion, he was neither man nor an animal and he used his nails and not a weapon to kill the asura. He laid Hiranyakasipu on his lap which is neither on earth, in the sky or water. The asura was slain at dusk when it is neither day nor night and on the threshold of the room which is neither inside nor outside a house. Vishnu had triumphed again over evil with the use of his supreme and subtle cleverness. Prahlada became the king and ruled with the blessings of Vishnu, restoring the age of good in the world.

Vamana Avatar

In his fifth avatar, Vishnu appears as a vamana, a dwarf. This is the first avatar in which he does not appear as an animal. As a matter of fact there is a logical progression of his avatars from an amphibious fish and tortoise to a boar, then a partial human in the man-lion and now to the dwarf. Their exploits are also all in the realms of the sky, underwater, and heavens. With the avatars that follow, Vishnu comes to earth as a man and all his actions also take place there.

The Vamana Avatar is the myth of the three cosmic steps and it is the first that can trace its origins to the Vishnu of the Vedas. The Rigveda speaks of the "three steps" of "Vishnu, the unconquerable preserver" who "strode over the universe". The first two steps covered the heavens, earth, and the netherworld and the third stepped into an eternity that only the sublime Vishnu could perceive. Another interpretation of the steps is of the earth where Vishnu is the fire; the atmosphere where he is lightning; and the third of the sky where he is the radiance of the sun.

The Vamana Avatar appears in the Treta Yuga, the second age of the earth. In this avatar Vishnu continues with his confrontation with the asura clan of Hiranyakasipu that began with his Varaha Avatar. Here he matches his wits with Bali who is the grandson of Prahlada and therefore the great-grandson of the Vishnu-hating Hiranyakasipu, who had been slain by the Narasimha Avatar to save Prahlada. This inter-weaving of the various myths of Vishnu is what adds an interesting dimension to the story of the avatars.

After the asuras lost the amrita to the gods in the myth of the Kurma Avatar, they became powerless. King Bali then performed great penances and gained a fabulous chariot, powerful weapons, and armour that made him invincible. He waged an endless war against the gods that he won and once again the asuras ruled over the three worlds. The gods, shorn of power prayed to the sage Rishi Kashyapa for guidance and he felt that only Vishnu could save them. Then Kashyapa's wife Aditi prayed that Vishnu should be born as her son and in this avatar he was born as a dwarf, a vamana.

As the son of Kashyapa and Aditi, the Vamana Avatar was a Brahmin and he went to the court of Bali who was busy performing a yajna. In spite of being an asura, Bali was a virtuous king like Prahlada and he offered great hospitality to Vishnu. Then with all the other Brahmins present there he offered Vishnu whatever he desired—a house, a village, gold, horses or elephants and he was surprised at Vishnu's modest request—he wanted the land that he could cover in three steps. An amused king looking at the small figure before him immediately granted his simple wish.

Then as Bali and his courtiers watched in amazement the dwarf figure began to grow until Vishnu had become an endless figure that pierced the sky. He took two steps—the first to cover the heavens and the next covered the earth and then Vishnu asked Bali what he should do. He had been promised three steps and all creation had been covered already. At this Bali offered his own head and as the Vamana stepped on him he was pushed down to Patala, the netherworld where he continued to rule as king.

Another early myth has Bali battling Indra and being slain by him. As Bali fell, a flood of jewels came out of his mouth. Indra then tore his body with his thunderbolt and as Bali, in spite of being an asura was a truly pure being, the various parts of his body produced different gems. His bones became diamonds, his eyes turned into sapphires, the rubies were his blood, the emeralds his marrow, the flesh were crystals and his teeth became pearls.

Near Chennai is the tiny hamlet of Mahabalipuram in Tamil Nadu where it is believed that the Vamana Avatar appeared before Bali. Here by the seashore are the rock cut caves and temples of the Pallava rulers and among the deities carved in the niches can be seen many of the avatars of Vishnu. The feat of the three eternal steps is known as Tripadavikrama and in many places carvings of these cosmic steps are worshipped in the shape of carvings of Vishnu's feet. The most famous is at the Vishnupada Temple at Gaya in Bihar and another is at the Manikarnika Ghat in Varanasi, Uttar Pradesh.

Parashurama Avatar

The sixth avatar of Vishnu is Parashurama, Rama with an axe, and he is the first incarnation of Vishnu who is said to have lived on earth and whose exploits all take place there. Parashurama is the first of three Rama avatars, the other two are Ramachandra of Ayodhya and Balarama, the brother of Krishna.

Parashurama was born a Brahmin, the son of the sage Rishi Jamadagni and his wife Renuka whose story can be found in both the Mahabharata and the Puranas. Vishnu took this avatar to wipe out the Kshatriya race from the face of the earth as this warrior class had become arrogant and tyrannical. Parashurama killed the race twenty-one times and the myth reflects a time in Hindu society when there was a fierce battle for supremacy between the priestly Brahmins and the Kshatriya kings.

Parashurama, a man of great willpower, was a devotee of Shiva. It was Shiva who had instructed him in the use of the Parasu, the battle axe, and given him his own weapon. Renuka, his mother, was born a princess and once when she went to bathe in the river she saw a king and his queens at play by the water and just for a moment she regretted her simple, spartan life in the hermitage. Jamadagni suspected his wife of entertaining impure thoughts and he ordered his sons to kill Renuka. The older sons refused to kill their mother and their furious father cursed them into becoming idiots. The youngest son, Parashurama, obeyed immediately and cut off his mother's head.

Pleased at such unquestioned obedience, Jamadagni wanted Parashurama to ask for three boons. Parashurama first asked that his mother should be restored to life with no memory of having being killed. Then, that all his brothers should be restored to their normal state. Finally he wanted to become invincible in battle and have the power to stay alive as long as he wanted. This last boon meant Parashurama was alive during the Ramayana and the Mahabharata and was an elder contemporary of two other Vishnu avatars of Rama and Krishna.

Parashurama's hostility to the Kshatriyas begins with a king named Kartavirya who had a thousand arms. Once Kartavirya paid a visit to Jamadagni's hermitage. The sage was not home but Kartavirya and his men were welcomed by Renuka and her sons and given all hospitality. However, when he was leaving the arrogant king took away the calf of the Kamadhenu cow that belonged to the ashram. An angry Parashurama went after the king and his men who were enjoying themselves felling trees and destroying the forest around the ashram. Kartavirya refused to return the calf and in the fight that followed Parashurama defeated and killed him.

Jamadagni felt that as a Brahmin, Parashurama should not have taken a life and sent his son off on a pilgrimage. While Parashurama was away, the sons of Kartavirya attacked the ashram and killed the defenceless Jamadagni and Renuka. Parashurama returned to find his parents murdered and desolation everywhere. He swore vengeance and vowed that he would wipe the race of Kshatriyas from the face of the earth. He had to do this twenty-one times because everytime some Kshatriya boys were hidden among other classes and they grew up, married Kshatriya women and continued the race. Finally when no Kshatriya male was left on earth, the women married Brahmin men and began a new race.

The mention of Parashurama is found in both the epics, where he is often depicted as a rather stubborn, quick tempered though high principled man. After his mighty feat of vengeance, Parashurama handed over the ashram to Rishi Kashyapa and retired to the mountains to meditate. Here he was visited by Arjuna and also Karna of the Mahabharata and he taught them to fight with the battle axe. He once fought a hard battle with Bhishma when both were badly wounded. In the Ramayana he was angered by Rama's breaking of Shiva's bow and invited Rama to a contest of arms. Rama defeated him and then spared his life as he was a Brahmin.

Traditionally the land of Malabar is said to have been created by Parashurama when he drove back the ocean and created the hills of the Ghat by cutting the earth with his axe. Parashurama obviously fascinated the writers of the Puranas who have created a many faceted character that combines, as historian Sukumari Bhattacharji notes, "The accepted Kshatriya values of courage, heroism and the militant temperament" and "the wrath and zeal of a mortified Brahmin. The result is an impressive hero."

Rama Avatar

Ramachandra, king of Ayodhya, is the seventh avatar of Vishnu and one of the hero-king-warrior incarnations of the god. The other being Krishna, the Yadava king of Mathura and Dwarka. Rama's myth is placed in the Treta Yuga, the second age of the earth and he was born in the royal Kshatriya caste of the solar race of the Suryavanshi. His story does get mentioned in the Mahabharata but it is the epic Ramayana that gives the most comprehensive account of the life and exploits of the ideal man and king named Ramachandra.

In the beginning the bards of ancient India sang of the exploits of a warrior-king called Rama who rescued his wife from a demon king. From village to village, town palace to temple precinct they carried the tale of Rama's love for his wife Sita and his epic battle with an evil king of Lanka called Ravana. Then as it happens with legends that are transmitted orally from one generation to another, Rama's legend too gathered its own myths and cultic stories. And over the centuries Rama, once a legendary king and warrior, became deified into a god-king who as an avatar of Vishnu came to earth to vanquish the forces of evil.

Through the ages Rama has become the embodiment of dharma for Hindus and as the inspiring symbol of goodness and duty he has won a unique place in the hearts of the people. He is the valiant warrior and benevolent king, the epitome of honour and duty as son, brother and husband and unlike the more complex and worldly Krishna, he remains the ideal human being. Among the avatars of Vishnu it is Rama and Krishna who became the inspiration for the devotional movement of Bhakti and inspired the great surge of mystical poetry across the country.

Like all the avatars of Vishnu, Rama was born at a time when evil was on the rise on this earth. The demon king, Ravana, had performed many severe penances and gained the boons of invincibility from Brahma. Like earlier asura kings he had become a menace to the gods and the sages and as the gods had failed to defeat this mighty king of Lanka, they appealed to Vishnu for help. They said that only he possessed the powers to nullify the boons of Brahma and it was time again for Vishnu to descend to earth as an avatar to vanquish the growing evil and iniquity. To do this, Vishnu chose to be born as the eldest son of King Dasaratha of Ayodhya.

As King Dasaratha was childless, he decided to perform the aswamedha yajna, the horse sacrifice, to propitiate the gods. During the yajna Vishnu appeared at the ceremony as a Brahmin and gave a pot of nectar to the king saying that the queens were to drink it. Dasaratha had three wives— Kaushalya, Kaikeyi, and Sumitra but he divided the nectar into two and gave half each to Kaushalya and Kaikeyi. At this Sumitra also begged for some and the two queens shared their nectar with her. Kaushalya gave birth to the eldest son, Ramachandra; Kaikeyi to Bharat and Sumitra had twin sons—Laxman and Shatrughna.

It was a carefree childhood for the four brothers as they grew up in Ayodhya, learning the art of war and kingship. Laxman was specially close to Rama while Bharat and Shatrughna were the best of friends. Rama was a sweet tempered, kind, caring prince and particularly beloved of the people of the kingdom and it was accepted that one day he would ascend the throne. When the boys were fifteen, the sage Rishi Vishwamitra came to Ayodhya seeking the help of Dasaratha against some demons who were harassing the sages in the forest. He wanted Rama and his brothers to go back with him to fight the demons and Dasaratha reluctantly agreed to let them go. Rama and Laxman fought the rakshasas and killed a fierce female rakshasi called Taraka. Vishwamitra then took the brothers under his wing, teaching them the holy books and also training them in the use of weapons.

Vishwamitra travelled with the four Ayodhya princes to the kingdom of Mithila. Here King Janaka was offering the hand in marriage of his beautiful daughter, the princess Sita. As he had found the baby girl while ploughing a field, she was named Sita, "furrow", and was believed to be the daughter of the earth goddess, Prithivi. All the great kings and princes were keen to win Sita's hand but Janaka had one condition they had to fulfill. Sita would marry the man who could bend Janaka's giant bow and put the bowstring on it. This bow had once belonged to Shiva himself and one prince after another tried and failed to even lift it. Then it was Rama's turn and not only did he bend it, he broke it into two pieces. Sita was married to Rama and his three brothers were also wed to three other Mithila princesses.

All Ayodhya was delighted to hear that Dasaratha was planning to anoint Rama as his heir apparent and if there was any anger and resentment it was only in the heart of Queen Kaikeyi. The crisis in the royal family began when Kaikeyi's maid, the malicious, hunch-backed Manthara provoked her mistress into trying to gain the throne for her son Bharat. Kaikeyi, who was the favourite of the king, in a show of anger entered the room of discontent, the Goshaghar, and locked herself inside. When Dasaratha went in to meet his queen, she reminded him of a time when she had saved his life on a battlefield and he had promised her a boon. Dasaratha promised her anything she wanted and then Kaikeyi came up with her pitiless request. She wanted her son Bharat to become the next king and Rama be sent into exile for fourteen years.

A heartbroken Dasaratha was distraught and at his units end. As a king he was bound to keep his promise but as a father he was unable to deprive his son of his right to the throne. Rama, hearing of his father's terrible dilemma, decided to leave the kingdom immediately and Sita and Laxman insisted on going with him. There is a beautiful passage in the Ramayana in which Rama tries to dissuade his gently nurtured young bride from accompanying him, warning her of the hardships and dangers of a life in the wilderness and Sita's confident, loving reply.

"Whether it is in ascetism, a hermitage, or in heaven, I want to be with you." says the constant Sita. "I can never be tired walking after you. The reeds, the grass, the thorny bushes on the way will seem to me in your company as soft to the touch as a lawn or the skin of an antelope."

"The dust thrown up by the wind to cover me will seem, dear husband, rich sandal-wood powder. With you it is heaven, away from you, hell. So it is. Be certain of it, O Rama, and be perfectly happy with me."

In spite of his mother's ambitions Bharat was himself unwilling to take the throne but Dasaratha could not break his word. As all Ayodhya mourned, Rama accompanied by faithful Sita and Laxman left for fourteen years of exile. They began to live near some hermitages in the Dandaka forest between the Godavari and the Yamuna rivers at a place called Chitrakoot. Here the three of them who had grown up in palaces, lived like forest dwellers in simple thatched huts and as the men went hunting for food, Sita foraged for fruits, berries, and herbs. The rishis in the ashrams were greatly pleased by their presence as the brothers protected them from the roving bands of rakshasas.

In Ayodhya a heart-broken Dasaratha died and Bharat hastened to Chitrakoot to beg his brother to return. His efforts were to no avail as Rama resolutely refused to break the promise that he had made to his father. Bharat refused to become king and Rama felt that it was his duty to complete the sentence that had been laid on him. After a long argument a compromise was reached when Bharat agreed to rule as a regent and he carried back a pair of Rama's shoes that he placed on the throne to symbolise his presence in Ayodhya.

After ten years at Chitrakoot, Rama, Sita, and Laxman visited the Rishi Agastya at his hermitage near the Vindhya mountains. The sage suggested that they come and live by the banks of the Godavari at a place called Panchavati. The Panchavati forest was often invaded by bands of troublesome rakshasas who raided the ashrams and among them was the fearful demoness Surpanakha who was the sister of Ravana, the king of Lanka.

One day Surpanakha saw the handsome Rama and immediately fell in love with him. She took the form of a beautiful woman to attract him but when Rama rejected her advances, she attacked Sita in a jealous rage and Laxman coming to Sita's defence cut off Surpanakha's nose and ears. Insulted, mutilated, and humiliated, the rakshasi now wanted only revenge and invaded Panchavati with a rakshasa army led by her brothers Khara and Dushana and in the battle that followed, Ram and Laxman decimated them. Maddened with rage, Surpanakha then flew to Lanka to complain to her powerful brother Ravana. At his court she told her tale of her humiliation and begged for revenge. To entice him further she tempted him with descriptions of the sublime beauty of Sita.

Ravana with his assistant Marich rode his flying chariot to Panchavati, where by the magic of maya, Marich turned himself into a beautiful golden deer with silver spots and wandered around the hut where Sita lived. She was so delighted with the deer's beauty that she wanted it as a pet and begged Rama to get it for her. Rama decided to humour his wife but Laxman stayed behind to guard Sita. As Marich tried to escape from Rama who was chasing him he was killed by Rama's arrow and just before dying he spoke in Rama's voice, calling for Laxman to come to his help. Hearing this Sita was convinced that Rama was in danger and wanted Laxman to go to his aid.

Even though Laxman was reluctant to leave her alone, an anxious Sita insisted that he should go to Rama's aid. So before leaving he drew a circle around the hut with his bow with the request that Sita should not step outside it as it was the Lakshman-rekha and the rakshasas would not be able to cross the magic protective line. Once Laxman left, Ravana in the guise of an ascetic came to beg at the hut and when Sita came out to give him a bowl of grain he moved away from the circle to entice her to walk further. The trusting Sita forgot Laxman's request and stepped across the protective Lakshman-rekha and was instantly captured by Ravana.

Ravana dragged Sita into his flying chariot and took flight and as she cried out for help a giant bird named Jatayu heard her and tried to save her. A bird against a demon—it was an unequal battle and the valiant Jatayu was mortally wounded by Ravana and fell to the ground. As the chariot flew towards Lanka a desperate Sita began to drop pieces of her jewellery along the way hoping the brothers would be able to track her through them. Then once they arrived in Lanka she stoutly refused every enticement from Ravana to marry him; he even offered to make her his queen. On hearing Sita's vehement protests, the angry king then imprisoned her in a grove of Ashoka trees, the Ashokavana.

Meanwhile in Panchavati, Rama and Laxman came back to discover that Sita was missing. Nearly mad with grief Rama wandered through the forest calling out to her. They came upon the dying Jatayu who told them of the abduction. The brothers immediately headed out towards Lanka. On the way they entered Pampa, the kingdom of the Vanars, the race of monkeys, where they met the Vanar king, Sugriva, and his commander Hanuman. These two vanars had found some of the jewellery that Sita had dropped on the way to Lanka to indicate her path, and they showed them to Rama. Sugriva had been dethroned by his brother Bali and Rama and Laxman helped him recover the throne by killing Bali.

Once he was king again, Sugriva offered his help in finding Sita and sent out his army in all directions to search for her. Hanuman, who chose to travel alone, headed towards the south and it was he who found Ravana's hidden fortress of Lanka. Hanuman was the son of Vayu, the god of the winds, and could leap and fly across huge distances. Reaching the ocean at the southern tip of the Indian peninsula he took a giant leap across the waters and arrived in Lanka, where he turned himself into a tiny monkey and succeeded in entering the Lanka fortress undetected.

When Hanuman arrived at the Ashoka grove he found Sita sitting despondently weeping under a tree and he tried to reassure her with the news of Rama. Sita meeting an amazing talking monkey swooned in fear and was only revived when Hanuman identified himself as a messenger of Rama by showing her his ring. He then offered to carry her back to safety but Sita refused as she would not touch another man and preferred to wait for Rama to come and rescue her.

On his way out Hanuman destroyed much of the Ashokavana and was captured by the guards and taken to the court of Ravana. The rakshasas angered by his defiance set fire to his tail but instead of being hurt Hanuman used his tail like a flaming torch to burn Lanka to ashes in the episode called the Lanka Dahan.

Hanuman returned to report everything to Rama and at this point Vibhishana, who was one of the younger brothers of Ravana, abandoned Lanka and joined Rama. The monkey army reached the edge of the ocean, across the waters was Lanka but they had no way to cross it. Rama begged the ocean to give way but when the ocean refused to respond an angry Rama picked up an arrow and pronounced a powerful mantra that would make it dry up the ocean. The sky darkened in fear and the ocean god rose to the surface to tell Rama that as an ocean it was his nature to flow and he could not move away and the only solution was for them to build a bridge. Rama was to get Nala, the son of Vishwakarma, to help him and the ocean would support the bridge on its waters. Led by Nala the monkey army got to work, carrying boulders and tree trunks and built a bridge called Ramasetu that was so well made it looked like a parting in the hair of the ocean.

In Lanka, Ravana was ready for war with his giant brother Kumbhakarna and son Indrajeet and an army of rakshasas. The Vanar and the rakshasa armies were pitted against each other on the battlefield and it was a ferociously fought battle where many monkeys were killed and even Rama and Laxman were wounded. When Laxman was hit by the magic arrow of Indrajeet called Shaktishel and fell unconscious,

Hanuman flew to the Gandhamadan mountain in the Himalayas to look for the Mrita Sanjivini herb that could save him. As time was running out, in his hurry Hanuman found it simpler to carry the whole mountain back with him and Laxman was revived once again. The battle continued—first Kumbhakarna and then Indrajeet were slain and then the mighty Ravana came out to fight.

In his classic Ramcharitmanas, the poet-saint Tulsidas described Rama's radiant beauty on the battlefield as he prepared to face Ravana,

> "There on the field of battle Rama's limbs were beautiful with the beauty of many loves. The crown of knotted hair on his head, with flowers intertwined, was very lovely, as when among the lightning flashes stars glitter on the purple hills. With his arms he twirled his bow and arrows and drops of blood were on his body, as beautiful as flocks of rayamuni birds perched happily on a tamala tree."

In the final battle as Rama and Ravana faced each other the demon king appeared with ten heads and twenty arms flashing weapons and everytime Rama cut off one head another appeared in its place. It was a fight to death between two of the greatest warriors of the time and as Ravana roared like a mighty lion, the sky was darkened by the flying arrows. Then Rama picked up an arrow gifted to him by Rishi Agastya, it moved like the wind with its point flaring with the fire of the sun and it was as weighty as the Mount Mandara. Rama first powered it with sacred mantras, then fitted it to his bow and then bending the bow to his chest he let the arrow fly. The arrow streaked across the air, pierced Ravana's chest and then dripping with his blood once more returned to Rama's quiver.

As the gods sent down a rain of flowers and the victorious army celebrated, Rama asked Brahma to revive all the vanars who had died in battle. Sita was rescued and after placing Vibhishana on the throne of Lanka, the victorious army headed for home. However, there was great disquiet in Rama's mind because he began to suspect Sita's virtue as she had been the captive of another man. When all her entreaties and explanations failed, a heartbroken Sita only wanted to die and asked Laxman to build a funeral pyre for her. She entered this ordeal by fire and such was her purity that Agni, the god of fire himself appeared to escort her through it unscathed. Rama, Sita, and Laxman then returned to Ayodhya on the flying chariot, the pushpaka ratha and the people of Ayodhya, delirious with joy at their safe return welcomed them by lighting oil lamps.

Rama was anointed king. He was a just and benevolent ruler but Sita's captivity at Lanka continued to haunt their lives. The subjects were unhappy with Rama for taking Sita back after she had lived in the home of another man and Rama, a dutiful king, believed that the trust of his people came before his personal happiness. So even though Sita was pregnant he left her at the ashram of the sage Rishi Valmiki. Here Sita gave birth to twin sons—Luv and Kusha—and Valmiki brought up the boys, teaching them all the skills of the Kshatriyas.

When the boys were fifteen, Rama held an ashwamedha yajna and the sacred white horse was let loose to wander. The boys caught the horse and refused to free it. At which Rama's three brothers came to fight them and they were all defeated by the boys. Hearing of two teenage ashram boys who defeated his army, Rama finally appeared at the battlefield and recognising his sons, he invited them to come to Ayodhya.

Valmiki persuaded a reluctant Sita to forgive her husband and accompany the boys and they arrived at Rama's court. Here before a gathering of the people of Ayodhya, Sita once again declared her innocence and then asked her mother Prithivi to come to her aid. As Rama and his court watched in horror, the earth under Sita's feet split open and she vanished into the kind lap of mother earth. Rama losing his wife forever had no wish to rule any longer. He put his sons on the throne and entered the waters of the Sarayu river which welcomed him and transported him to heaven.

The epic Ramayana was written around the 5th century BC in Sanskrit and is credited to Rishi Valmiki. "The hero created by Valmiki", says historian Sylvain Levi, "still remains for contemporary India the most perfect model of humanity. Rama's peaceable courage, always at the service of virtue, his passionate devotion to duty, his fine delicate sensibility, his filial piety, his conjugal tenderness, the communion of his spirit with all Nature, are traits of eternal beauty which time can neither destroy nor weaken."

The Ramayana is called Adi Kavaya, the first poem, and is divided into seven books—Balakanda, Ayodhyakanda, Aranyakanda, Kishkindhakanda, Sundarakanda, Yuddhakanda, and Uttarakanda. In its present form it has 24,000 shlokas. It is a complex literary creation of innumerable myths and stories and only the outline of Rama's tale can be given here. This eternal tale has all the elements that make a great epic—martial adventures, romantic love, royal intrigue and ultimately personal tragedy—and has mesmerised people for centuries. Even today when the Ramleela folk plays enact Rama's story, the response of the crowds is charged with worship and emotion.

Scholars feel that Book One and Seven in which Rama is called an avatar were added much later. In the earliest form of the legend he has no divine attributes. His cult developed after that of Krishna though he is believed to be an earlier avatar. These legends of the life of a king of Ayodhya have inspired poets and playwrights, painters and musicians for centuries. Over the years many versions of the epic have been produced and among them the most popular is the Ramcharitmanas of Tulsidas. The poet-saint Tulsidas who lived during Mughal times rendered the tale in the vernacular Hindi which brought the epic within the reach of common people. To this day, his exquisite verses are read by people in North India as a part of their daily worship.

In his images Rama is depicted as a handsome, dark hued man carrying a bow and arrow with Sita and Laxman beside him. Sometimes he is dressed simply in the clothes of a forest dweller, at others he is a magnificent king, resplendent in silks and jewels. Sita as an incarnate of Lakshmi is an ideal beauty and Rama's reign is called Ramarajya, the ideal kingship. For centuries Rama's devotion to duty, the fidelity of Sita and the loyalty of Laxman and Hanuman have been regarded as religious and ethical ideals. Places connected to their lives like Ayodhya, Chitrakoot, and Rameshwaram have become important pilgrimages. There are temples dedicated to them in every village and town in the land and many festivals are celebrated around episodes of their lives.

Among the most important festivals are Ramanavami that celebrates the birth of Rama. Then on Dussehra night giant effigies of Ravana, Kumbhakarna, and Indrajeet go up in a shower of sparkling fireworks to celebrate the day when Rama killed the king of Lanka. On Deepavali people decorate their homes with lamps in the same way as the people of Ayodhya had welcomed their beloved prince. Bengal celebrates Durga Puja on the days when Rama had worshipped the warrior goddess asking for her blessings before attacking Lanka. For Hindus everywhere, Rama, Sita, Laxman, and Hanuman are an indelible part of their spiritual existence.

Krishna Avatar

Krishna, the king of Mathura and Dwarka is the eighth avatar of Vishnu and one of his most popular and worshipped incarnations. Like Rama, he was a warrior and king who ruled in the Gangetic plain and over the centuries he became deified as an avatar. The epic Mahabharata, in which Krishna plays a pivotal role, mentions Rama and so it can be presumed that Rama had lived before Krishna. Like Rama, his legend begins with a victory in a war, though Krishna's role as a warrior is more complex as it is combined with those of a philosopher and statesman. And like Rama, his myth spans his complete life from birth to death.

Krishna, the 'dark one', is by far the most complex, intricately imagined and surprisingly human of the Vishnu avatars. His cult, the sect of the Vaishnavas, worship him not just as a man but also as a child, the handsome lover, the benevolent king, the invincible warrior, and finally the philosopher. Then through his words spoken in the Bhagavad Gita, Hindus gained a set of religious and ethical teachings that have guided their spiritual and temporal lives for centuries. Amazingly, it is relevant even today as the simple and practical words of the Gita have the suppleness of thought that continues to provide a way to face the dilemmas of modern life.

The name of Krishna is first found in the Chandogya Upanishad where a scholar named Krishna, son of Devaki is mentioned. Krishna's life and exploits as a king can be found in the Mahabharata but by the time the Harivamsa and the Bhagavad Purana were written, he had been transformed into a divine Supreme Being. Like Rama, he was the inspiration of the mystic Bhakti movement and poet-saints like the Alvars, Mirabai, Surdas and Jaidev have sung his praises in immortal verse. Meera's bhajans, the Alvar hymns, Jaidev's exquisite *Gita Govinda* and *Prem Sagar* which is the Hindi version of the Bhagavad Purana, are woven into the traditions of Vaishnava worship. As Mirabai sang of her dark hued lord,

> "I'm coloured with the colour of dusk, O Rana
> Coloured with the colours of my Lord.
> Drumming out the rhythms on the drums, I danced,
> Dancing in the presence of the saints, Coloured with
> the colours of my Lord."

Krishna's story begins in the kingdom of Mathura where the king Ugrasen was deposed and imprisoned by his son, the cruel and tyrannical Kansa. Ugrasen also had a daughter named Devaki who was married to Vasudev. Kansa was an evil king and his avarice and oppression of the people got so unbearable that the earth goddess Prithivi herself went to the gods begging for succour. The gods then prayed to Vishnu, reminding him of his promise that he would come down to earth whenever evil began to rise and righteousness had to be established. This time Vishnu chose to be born in the home of the oppressor himself, as a child of Devaki and Vasudev.

One day when Devaki and Vasudev were travelling in a chariot with Kansa, a voice spoke from the sky saying that the eighth child of Devaki would one day kill Kansa. He immediately drew out his sword to kill his sister but Vasudev came between them and then to save his wife he made a desperate promise. Vasudev said that he would personally bring every child born to Devaki to Kansa and if the king wanted, he could kill them. Momentarily satisfied by this terrible assurance Kansa spared his sister's life but he put her and Vasudev in a prison.

Everytime a child was born to Devaki, Vasudev would carry the new born baby to Kansa, who would mercilessly murder it. Then on a moonless, monsoon night Devaki gave birth to her eighth child, a boy, and Vasudev decided to try and save the child. It was past midnight, the guards were dozing over their spears as Vasudev carried the baby through the prison. No one saw him and then as the barred doors and gates miraculously opened, he walked out of the palace. It was raining heavily when he reached the banks of the river Yamuna but the waters of the river sank below his knees and he crossed over. He entered the home of a cowherd named Nanda, whose wife Yashoda had given birth to a daughter.

As the world slept, Vasudev exchanged the babies and returned to the prison. The guards woke to the sound of a baby crying and ran to call Kansa who came rushing in. He picked up the infant girl and flung her against a wall but the child flew away with a laugh and before she vanished, she predicted that the one he wanted to kill was still alive and would one day come to take revenge. Kansa freed Vasudev and Devaki as he felt that they were no longer a threat to him but then sent out his soldiers to kill every newborn child in Mathura. Vasudev hurried to Nanda's house and suggested that he and his family should flee to the village of Gokul. He also gave his son Balarama, who was the child of his second wife, to Nanda so that the two brothers could grow up together.

Krishna and Balarama grew up in Gokul and then Vrindavan and there are many stories of the child's superhuman qualities. Kansa sent many demons to kill him but little Krishna vanquished them all. Among them was Putana, a demoness with poisoned breasts who had killed many newborn children but when she offered her breast to Krishna, he sucked out her life and himself remained unharmed. Krishna was a naughty child who often stole butter from the kitchen and once an angry Yashoda tied him to a heavy wooden mortar and when Krishna dragged it outside, it got wedged between two trees and he pulled so hard that the trees were uprooted.

Krishna lived like the other cowherd boys, taking the cattle out to the pastures, where he played his flute and then in the evening he would bring them back again. He was still a child when a giant serpent named Kaliya began to poison the waters of the Yamuna. The cows that drank the water began to die and the trees by the river banks all withered. Then Krishna waded into the river and after a mighty battle he defeated the snake but instead of killing him, he allowed it to escape to the sea.

Once Krishna challenged the king of the gods Indra himself. The cowherds were preparing to worship Indra as the god of rain and Krishna convinced them that they should make their offerings to the Govardhana hill instead, as their cows were fed by the green pastures on the slopes of the hill. As the cowherds prayed to the hill, Krishna appeared on the summit to receive their offerings. An angry Indra sent down a deluge of rain to drown everyone. Krishna raised the Govardhana hill by one hand and the people sheltered under it for seven days and nights, until Indra's wrath had cooled down. Krishna's legends tell of many childhood pranks like hiding the clothes of the milkmaids, the gopis, who were bathing in the river and mighty deeds of slaying the demons sent by Kansa.

As Krishna grew into a handsome young man all the gopis, the wives, and daughters of the cowherds fell in love with him. They would watch by their windows, waiting for Krishna to pass by and at the sound of his flute they would leave everything to go out to meet him. As they all wanted to dance with him at the same time, Krishna would transform himself into many so that each had a Krishna to dance the Rasleela.

Among the gopis his favourite was Radha, the wife of
Ayanagosha who lived in the nearby village of Barsana.

The romance of Radha and Krishna has remained the
romantic ideal of his worshippers and some of the most
lyrical poetry has been written around the subject of this
divine love. In the temples, it is Radha who receives worship
beside him instead of his two queens Rukmini and
Satyabhama. The call of Krishna's flute is the call to divine
love and enlightenment and the mystic poetess Andal
describes the feelings of the gopis,

> Eternal Mathura's wonder-child,
> Chief of Yamuna's holy tract,
> Jewelled lamp of the cowherd clan,
> Damodara, a revelation to his mother.
> If we, unsullied, adore him with flowers,
> Sing full-throated and give him our thoughts,
> All our sins, past and future
> Like cotton in a fire, will be burnt away!

The attempts on his life continued all this while. Krishna
and Balarama then heard that Kansa was holding a sporting
contest at Mathura. When the two young men arrived at the
sporting arena they were recognised by Kansa who sent his
wrestlers and elephants to kill them. The two brothers
defeated them all and then Krishna sprang up to confront
Kansa himself and after a fierce fight he killed him. He then
freed Ugrasen and reinstated him on the throne. The brothers
stayed on at Mathura where subsequently Krishna was
crowned king.

Krishna was a great king, wise and benevolent and there was happiness and prosperity in the kingdom. However, Mathura was often at war because of his many enemies. The greatest danger came from Jarasandha, the king of Magadha, who had vowed revenge as two of his daughters had been married to Kansa. He attacked Mathura eighteen times and even though Krishna defeated him everytime, the people were exhausted by this constant state of war. Then danger appeared from another quarter with the invasion of Kalayavahan, the king of the Yavanas. So Krishna decided that his people would be safer in another place and built a new kingdom in the west by the sea, with a fabulous new capital he named Dwarka.

Kalyavahan refused to give up and chased Krishna to Dwarka and his army surrounded the city. Krishna came out alone to confront him and then making sure Kalayavahan saw him, he raced away from the city on his chariot, luring the enemy into the hills. He climbed into the hills and hid inside a cave. Kalayavahan saw him enter the cave and climbed up to find a man asleep at the mouth of a cave. Thinking the man was Krishna he kicked the sleeping figure and was instantly burnt to ashes. This man was Muchkunda who had received a boon from the gods that he could sleep forever and whoever tried to wake him against his will would be turned into ashes. Many of the myths of Krishna show this ability to mix clever stratagems with courage to gain his ends.

As king of Dwarka, Krishna acquired three chief wives—Rukmini, Satyabhama, and Jambavati. The Puranas of course credit him with sixteen thousand wives and one lakh eighty thousand sons! Like all legendary heroes these marriages were not mere alliances but also romantic adventures. Rukmini was the princess of Vidarbha who had fallen in love with Krishna but she was betrothed to Sisupala, the king of Chedi. Krishna carried her off just before her wedding and thus made a lifelong enemy of Sisupala. The enmity only ended with his death at Krishna's hands.

Satyabhama was the daughter of a Yadava chief named Satrajit who possessed a rare jewel called Syamantaka. When Satrajit heard that Krishna coveted this jewel, he gave it to his brother Prasena to hide but then Prasena was killed in a forest by a lion. Jambavat, the king of the bears killed the lion and found the gem in its mouth. Satrajit, however, suspected Krishna of killing his brother for the jewel and to clear his name Krishna tracked the path of Prasena into the forest, fought Jambavat, and recovered the Syamantaka. Being a shrewd king he allied with both the powerful chieftains by marrying Satyabhama, the daughter of Satrajit and Jambavati, the daughter of Jambavat. Rukmini was the mother of his son Pradyumna and daughter Charumati and his son Samba was born of Jambavati.

The history of Krishna the king is to be found in the Mahabharata where he allies himself with the five Pandava brothers of Indraprastha against their cousins the Kauravas of Hastinapur. In the great battle that follows, Krishna's guidance and strategic thinking help the Pandavas to triumph over their enemies. In the Mahabharata Krishna is not treated as a god but as one of the greatest kings of the time whose alliance is sought by both sides.

In the Mahabharata, Krishna first appears among the royal guests at the swayamvara ceremony of Draupadi where

Arjuna wins her as his bride. This is the beginning of his friendship with Arjuna that lasts their lifetimes and is one of the highlights of the epic. Krishna becomes a friend, ally, and mentor of the Pandavas and is present at all the pivotal moments of their lives. In the earliest versions of the Mahabharata, Krishna is still a great hero, warrior and king and like all the other characters he is human. Unlike the Ramayana he is not a deified avatar of Vishnu and there are no monkey armies and rakshasas in this secular epic. These changes appear in the later additions of the Harivamsa, the Bhagavad Gita and also the Bhagavad and the Vishnu Puranas.

The alliance with the Pandavas is also of great benefit to Krishna. Accompanied by Arjuna and Bhima he confronts his biggest enemy Jarasandha and Bhima challenges Jarasandha to a wrestling match and kills him. They then free the kings who had been imprisoned by the tyrannical king. Krishna helps Arjuna in eloping with his sister Subhadra even though brother Balarama does not approve. Then at the Rajasuya sacrifice of Yudhishtira, Krishna kills Sisupala with his sudarshana chakra when Sisupala challenges and abuses him.

At the gambling match where Yudhishthira lost his kingdom and then wagered and lost his wife, it is Krishna who came to the aid of Draupadi. The Pandavas sat like spineless cowards as Draupadi was dragged into court and publicly humiliated by Dushasana who pulled at her clothes. She cried out to Krishna to help and he kept renewing her sari as fast as Dushasana tore at it until the latter was exhausted and gave up.

The Pandavas went into exile and as war became imminent Krishna tried his best to achieve a reconciliation but failed because of the arrogance of the Kauravas. Both Duryodhana and Arjuna went to Dwarka seeking Krishna's support. Krishna said that he would not personally fight but would offer his services as a charioteer and they had a choice between him and his army. As Arjuna chose Krishna, Duryodhana was quite happy to get Krishna's vast Narayani army.

On the battlefield of Kurukshetra, it was the first day of the war and the two armies were ranged against each other. Arjuna looked across at the enemy and they were all his friends and relatives—a beloved grandfather, respected teachers, cousins he had grown up with and he faced a profound moral dilemma. His heart filled with sadness, he laid down his bow and refused to fight. At which Krishna, the charioteer spoke the words of the Bhagavad Gita that teach of the duties of a person and the concept of Karma Yoga, a subtle and at times abstruse path of action,

> "Just as the unwise act, being attached to their action, even so should the wise act, O Bharata, but without attachment, and only with a view to promoting the solidarity of society."

Then Krishna urged Arjuna to do his duty as a warrior without thinking of the consequences of his actions. The Gita speaks of dutifulness combined with detachment and equanimity, what Krishna called nishkama karma—a dispassionate considered action without any expectations of the returns.

"Renouncing into Me all actions, with your mind fixed on the Self, and becoming free from desire and all sense of 'my-ness', do you fight, freed from your spiritual fever."

For as Krishna said, death is inevitable but the true self or atman is eternal, so a battle is just another act of karma. His own life was not always a perfect example of this calm uninvolvement but he was oddly untouched by both the triumphs and defeats he had to face.

During the battle, though he did not fight himself, Krishna was of invaluable service to the Pandavas. However, on two occasions he gave advice for actions which were not ethical. First he advised Yudhishthira to lie about the death of Asvatthama, the son of the Kaurava general Dronacharya. This led to Dronacharya losing heart and he was killed. Then during the fight between Bhima and Duryodhana he advised Bhima to hit Duryodhana below the navel and break his thighs, a move that was not allowed in a duel using gadas, the ancient maces.

Once the Pandavas were in power in Hastinapur, Krishna returned to Dwarka but his last days were darkened by hopelessness and tragedy. As he watched in horror, the men of his Yadava clan became steeped in debauchery and Krishna had to ban the drinking of wine. However, he allowed the serving of wine at festivals. He saw his decadent clansmen fight and kill each other in a drunken brawl. After his son Pradyumna was killed before his eyes, Krishna and Balarama withdrew into a forest where the injured Balarama died first and a white serpent escaped from his mouth as he was the avatar of Vishnu's snake, Sheshnaga.

Krishna the invincible warrior had one vulnerable spot in his body because of an old curse by Rishi Durvasas and this was his left heel. As he sat in the forest contemplating the tragic end of his great kingdom, he sat with his left foot resting on his knee. A hunter named Jara mistook him for a deer and his arrow hit Krishna's heel. Before he died, Krishna forgave Jara and his words of consolation and forgiveness for the grieving hunter were the last ones that he spoke on this earth. Then Krishna rose to heaven and was once again merged into the radiance of Vishnu.

The two hero-avatars of Vishnu—Rama and Krishna—both have lives that move through great upheavals of triumphs and adversities and have epic tragic ends. Both began as heroes of the martial songs of the balladeers and as their legends grew they acquired the halo of being the incarnations of Vishnu. In the Mahabharata, Krishna is more of a shrewd, visionary king who makes sure his side wins. He is remote and regal, thoughtful and conniving, qualities that still fascinate thinkers and writers. He is unpredictable, volatile, with an ironic wit and he is far from perfect. This Krishna is mortal with human frailties but by the time of the Harivamsa and the Bhagavat Purana he had absorbed the beliefs of many local cults and the teachings of popular philosophers and become a god.

The Mahabharata gives no details of his childhood among the cowherds but the southern part of India had a cowherd god named Mayon, 'the dark one' who sported with milkmaids. The cult of this god was brought to the north-west by the pastoral tribe of the Abhiras and his playful life with the gopis became a part of the myth of Krishna. Some scholars feel that the teachings of a philosopher named Narayana, the son of Viswaka, were also incorporated into the beliefs of the Krishna cult. The teachings of the Gita are the result of a great stream of thought that was credited to Krishna and polished into one of the most profound treatises of Hindu thought. These verses of the Bhagavad Gita were added later to the tale of the great war and placing them beside the moral dilemma of Arjuna was an act of brilliant inspiration as it provided it with a great dramatic backdrop.

Krishna is believed to be the most complete manifestation of Vishnu and for his devotees he is a truly many faceted god. There is always some aspect of him that appeals to a devotee—the legendary hero, the divine lover, the playful child, king, statesman, thinker, mystic, and god. Krishna's immense and complex character encompasses every aspect of human experience and it is this vividness that has made him so popular. If Surdas sang of the butter stealing Govinda, for Mirabai and Andal he was their eternal lover and friend. For Chaitanya and Nityananda his teachings make him the source of all wisdom and enlightenment. All the classical dances of India depict his life while the folk songs of Thumri sing his legends. And through it all he remains complicated, vulnerable and a very human god whose myths are painted in both black and white.

Krishna has innumerable names. He is Govinda, the cowherd; Damodara because he dragged away the mortar tied to his belly; Gopal, Govardhana, Vasudeva and Bhagavat. Balarama, who carried a plough is called Haladhara and Sankarshana. Radha is believed to be an incarnation of Lakshmi. Krishna's icons reflect the many moods of this vibrant and colourful god. He is dark skinned, always benign and smiling, with perfect features and he wears a peacock feather in his hair. He is shown as the happy cowherd, playing the flute, with Radha beside him. He is depicted as a crawling child holding a ball of butter, a boy dancing on the hoods of the serpent Kaliya and holding up the Govardhana mountain. Krishna the king is a majestic standing figure, wearing much jewellery and a crown, clad in yellow-gold silk. At Puri he is worshipped as Jagannatha with his siblings Balarama and Subhadra.

The region of Mathura-Vrindavan is called Brajbhoomi and even today it sways in a loving worship of Krishna. Every hamlet from Gokul, Govardhana to Barsana has its own Krishna legend and there are temples everywhere. During the rule of Muslim kings, this region often faced the onslaught of their armies and all the old temples were destroyed. Many of the images were taken away by the rulers of nearby kingdoms and consecrated in new temples, like the Nathdwara Temple in Rajasthan and the Sakshi Gopal in Orissa. Among other important temples to Krishna are Dwarkadeesh in Gujarat, Srirangam in Tamil Nadu and Tirupati in Andhra Pradesh.

Janamashtami, Krishna's birthday, is one of the most important religious festivals of the Hindus. Temples in Brajbhoomi enact the folk drama of the Krishnaleela showing all his superhuman feats. The spring festival of Holi is also woven into the Krishna legend as he is said to have sprayed the gopis with colour. The most colourful carnivals take place at Vrindavan and Barsana in Uttar Pradesh. The Vaishnavas are among the largest sects in the land and among all the avatars of Vishnu, Krishna is the easiest to love and worship as he is the most human and accessible. He is compassionate and just, humorous and wise, and is also fierce in his defence of the good against evil. He is the ally when dharma is threatened and for his devotees Krishna is friend, guide and god.

Buddha Avatar

Gautama Buddha, the founder of Buddhism, is believed to be the ninth avatar of Vishnu. The inclusion of the teacher of a heterodox sect that was critical of the Brahmanical religion in the Vishnu pantheon often surprises people. The inclusion of the Buddha as an avatar is in fact a continuation of an old tradition of absorbing and redefining any cult or belief that rose to challenge the mainstream Hindu system. It had begun with the Dravidian Shiva, when the Puranas claimed him as a god and continued with the evolution of the Mother Goddess and local cults around the worship of snakes and monkeys.

What is most intriguing about the surprising choice of the Buddha as an avatar is the way myths were created to justify his inclusion, in spite of the fact that his teachings were critical of the role of the priesthood and of the caste system. It also reflects the Hindu tradition of worshipping whatever is good on this earth. A simple tolerance that makes them pray at Sufi shrines and go on pilgrimages on Urs festivals. It is this generous ability to absorb and transform that made Gautama Buddha an avatar of Vishnu.

The Buddha is a historical figure, he was born in 563 BC as Siddhartha Gautama, a prince of the Sakya clan. His father,

King Shuddhodhana, had been warned that his son could leave home as an ascetic and to stop this, he surrounded his son with all the luxuries of the palace. Protected and pampered, Siddhartha was married to a beautiful princess and had a son. However, when he was twenty-nine, while riding through the city in his chariot he saw things that deeply disturbed him. First he saw an old man walking with the aid of a stick, next a man dying by the roadside and then a dead man being carried for cremation. He thus became aware of the human burdens of old age, disease, and death. Finally, he saw a wandering holy man who looked at peace with himself and decided that the answer to his questions lay in contemplation.

Siddhartha left everything to wander as an ascetic seeking an answer to all the sorrows of life. In his search for enlightenment he took instructions from gurus and even performed such severe austerities that his body was emaciated and he was close to death. Then he rejected the path of asceticism and went back to contemplation at which five of his companions abandoned him. Finally he sat down to meditate under a peepal tree by the Nairanjana river in Bodh Gaya and after forty-nine days of meditation he gained enlightenment. He became the Buddha, "the one who is fully awake". The Buddha then travelled to a mango grove at Sarnath, near Varanasi, where he found his old companions and he gave his first sermon to them.

The Buddha's teachings are based on the four Noble Truths. First that life is rooted in dukkha, suffering. This suffering is caused by tanha, craving for power, pleasures and a long life. To be released from this craving is to be released from suffering. And the way to achieve this is through the

Noble Eight Fold path. This path is of right understanding, right intention, right speech, right action, right livelihood, right effort, right awareness, and right concentration. The Buddha was critical of the Hindu priestly caste of Brahmins and said that enlightenment was possible for everyone irrespective of their caste.

To transform the Buddha into an avatar, when he questioned both the caste system and the superiority of the priests who propagated and benefited from it, could not have been easy. The myths in the Puranas try rather ineffectually to prove that the Buddha taught a religion inimical to Brahmanism, deluding the wicked to deny the Vedas, so that the unrighteous who obeyed him could be revealed and could face the wrath of Vishnu. Even though the priests tried to propagate the worship of the Buddha Avatar, like at the Vihara at Bodh Gaya which was turned into a temple, it never gained the worship of the people.

The Skanda Purana gives a myth trying to explain why Vishnu became the Buddha Avatar and it clearly shows a time when the Shaivite religion was threatened in the city of Kashi by the teachings of the Buddha. Once the earth was stricken by a terrible famine that had lasted for seven years. Brahma then went to a king named Ripanjaya saying that the gods were not allowing the rains to fall on earth because the kings had become so wicked. Brahma wanted Ripanjaya to become the king of the world and he agreed on one condition, that all the gods would leave the earth and he could rule alone as long as righteousness prevailed there.

The gods left for heaven but Shiva was reluctant to leave his favourite earthly home, the city of Kashi (Varanasi) and

Brahma had to personally persuade him to do so. Ripanjaya then took the name of Divodasa and began to rule Kashi. The rains came and through his just and wise rule the earth was prosperous again. Shiva, however, still hankered for his beloved Kashi and he kept sending his messengers to find out if righteousness still prevailed there. To his disappointment, all his messengers were so happy in Kashi that they stayed on there and none of them returned to heaven.

Finally the gods appealed to Vishnu who came down to earth as the Buddha Avatar, to live near Kashi, at a place called Dharmakshetra. Lakshmi became one of his female disciples and Garuda was a pupil named Punyakriti. The Buddha Avatar denied the supremacy of the Vedas and said there were no gods like Shiva and Vishnu. He discouraged the performing of sacrifices as they achieved nothing and instead he encouraged a life of worldly pleasures. As the teachings of the Buddha Avatar became popular a disheartened Divodasa finally decided to abandon Kashi. He consecrated a Shiva lingam in the city and after making his son the next king he went to heaven and Shiva could once again return to Kashi.

The Shiva Purana tells the story of a teacher named Rishi Gautama and his wife Ahalya. The Rishi had performed great penances and gained the boon from Varuna of the most beautiful hermitage on earth. His ashram was a haven of spiritual contemplation, it was shaded by fruit bearing trees and its gardens were always filled with flowers. Here Gautama, Ahalya and their disciples lived in great peace and contentment.

Ahalya and the disciples once came into conflict with the Brahmin women of a nearby village who prevented them from bathing in the river. These women created further trouble by complaining to their husbands about the people in the ashram. The Brahmins prayed to Ganesha and begged him to free them from the presence of Gautama. Ganesha was reluctant but he had already promised a boon, so he took the form of an old cow and began to eat the crop in the ashram's rice field. Gautama wanting to drive away the cow hit it with a blade of grass and to his horror the cow fell down and died.

Gautama and Ahalya had to abandon the ashram because of the sin of killing a cow. A repentant Gautama then prayed to Shiva for many years and a pleased Shiva came down to tell him of how Ganesha was made to trick Gautama into abandoning his ashram. An angry Gautama then began to preach a religion that opposed the role of the priesthood and denied the sanctity of the Vedas.

There are many similar elements between the teachings of the Buddha and Hinduism, the most important is the common belief in reincarnation. Siddhartha Gautama is believed to be one in a long line of past Buddhas. The final Buddha who is yet to come is Maitreya and the Vishnu Avatars have a similar incarnation called Kalki. The myths of the Buddha Avatar are clearly the reaction of the old religion to a perceived threat from the more humane teachings of a great teacher. However, all the lists of the avatars of Vishnu do not include the Buddha. He is there in the list of the poet Jayadeva but in other compilations Krishna's brother Balarama is called an avatar of Vishnu.

Kalki Avatar

Kalki, the tenth and final avatar of Vishnu is the incarnation that is yet to come. When Krishna ascended to heaven, the Kali Yuga began. This is the final age on earth as it decays to its inevitable end at the completion of the four Yugas. Kalki would arrive on earth to end this final and degenerate age. After that a new cycle of Yugas will begin with the Krita or Satya Yuga, when righteousness and prosperity will once again prevail on earth.

Kalki, as an avatar that has not yet appeared, naturally has no myths but the Puranas are full of descriptions of the state of the earth when he will arrive. He will appear when falsehood and wickedness fills the earth and tyrannical kings rule everywhere who kill women, children, and cows. The worship of the gods will wane and the people will take refuge from their kings in the forests and live on wild honey, roots, fruits, flowers, and leaves.

The Kalki Avatar is depicted as a man riding a white horse and with a sword in his hand. Sometimes he is described as a giant with a horse's head. The Kalki Purana predicts that he would be born in a Brahmin family and will have superhuman qualities. He will annihilate the wicked, save the good and re-establish the rule of righteousness on earth. Brahma will then awake from his cosmic sleep to begin the work of creation and the next Krita Yuga will then begin.

CHAPTER NINE

Shiva

"To the utterly at one with Siva
There's no dawn, no new moon
No noonday, nor equinoxes
Nor sunsets, nor full moons
His front yard is the true Benaras
O Ramanatha !"
— Devara Dasimayya, 7th century Tamil poet

Shiva is Isvara, the great god and like Vishnu his worship reverberates across the land. As the third member of the divine trinity with Brahma and Vishnu he has the terrible role of the destroyer. Once the creation of Brahma has run its course and reached its final stage, Shiva destroys it all, so that the cycle of creation can start again. He dances the maddened cosmic dance of the Tandava and everything is demolished under his dancing feet. His third eye opens and its fierce rays all to ashes.

The sect that worships Shiva is called Shaivite and the temples to the god are to be found in every part of the country. The worship of Shiva is founded on surrender and asceticism and less on the tender devotion of the Vaishnavas. It appeals to the questioning and meditative mind and it is less bound by the rules of caste or religious rituals. As a matter of fact some of the greatest mystic-poets who wrote hymns to Shiva belonged to lower castes.

Another Shaiva cult is of the Tantric way of worship which is an obscure, rather esoteric sect that uses complex spells, sacred formulas and secret rituals known only to the initiates. Its worship includes both Shiva and his consort the Devi and offers salvation through this hidden, mysterious Tantric way. The Tantric also influenced a Buddhist sect and is popular in Tibet.

Shiva's devotees have ranged from kings to potters and hunters and among them the most famous are the Nayanmar poets of South India. Poets like Basavanna, Sambandar, Appar, and Sundarar sang to the many moods of this complex god, trying to capture his quicksilver character as they surrendered to the worship of Shiva. As Sambandar wrote in the seventh century,

> "The serpent is his ear stud, he rides a bull
> He is crowned with the pure white crescent
> He is smeared with the ashes of destroyed forests
> He is decked with a garland of full blossoming flowers
> When his devotees call him he comes glittering
> And bestows his grace upon all.
> He is indeed the thief who has stolen my soul away."

He is a contrary god, the lord of darkness and light, death and creation, a complex blend of compassion and quick anger, generosity and impatience. He is the god of the ascetics and also a family man married to Parvati. He can wander about wearing animal skins and adorn himself with silk and flowers. He is indifferent to pleasure but also a symbol of regeneration. He is the outcaste among the gods and the champion of the outsiders in human society, the people without status. He is often in a state of genial intoxication and can generate a mystic fervour in his devotees. Like a chameleon Shiva encompasses every human feeling and experience and that is why he is so beloved of his devotees.

Shiva is usually depicted as a wandering mendicant. He is dark skinned, wears a tiger skin and his bare body is smeared with the ash from cremation grounds. His matted locks are piled on top of his head and within his locks hides the river goddess Ganga, while the crescent moon glows above his forehead. Shiva wears a necklace of rudraksha beads and carries a small drum, the Damaru; a trident, the Trishula, and a begging bowl. The Trishula is his favourite weapon but he is also the divine archer and uses a giant bow called Pinaka.

Across his forehead are drawn the three stripes called the Tripundraka and in the centre is the third eye that symbolises wisdom and also anger. Snakes writhe around his neck like a living necklace and beside him sits his vehicle, the Nandi bull. He lives on Mount Kailash in the Himalayas and has no heavenly palaces, home is often in a cave or under shady trees. Sometimes, in a happier frame of mind Shiva dresses as a bridegroom in silks but even then unlike Vishnu he wears little jewellery. The simple mendicant is quite pleased wearing just a garland of fresh flowers and bilva leaves. He is an earthy god, in essence an ascetic and is never a resplendent king of the heavens like Vishnu.

As Sukumari Bhattacharji tries to discover Shiva's inexplicable attraction as a god, she writes, "He stands for supreme detachment as also for ritual abandon and indulgence. He is indifferent to worldly ties, yet he himself is the only god with a really convincing family. He lives both in cremation grounds and on a lofty mountain peak and is a friend of Kuvera, the god of wealth. He is dressed as a mendicant and is yet a giver of many gifts. Himself the object of meditation, he is ever lost in meditation."

One of the greatest bhaktas of Shiva was the mystic poet Basavanna, who called Shiva, "the lord of the meeting rivers" and tried to explain why he worshipped this volatile, impulsive but still merciful god,

> "How can I feel right
> About a god who eats up lacquer and melts
> Who wilts when he sees fire?
> How can I feel right
> `About gods you sell in your need,
> And gods you bury for fear of thieves?
> The Lord of the meeting rivers,
> Self-born, one with himself,
> He alone is the true god."

Vishnu was at least mentioned in the Vedas, Shiva does not appear at all in Vedic literature. His beginnings are traced to an obscure Vedic god called Rudra who had just two and a half hymns dedicated to him. Shiva does share many of the elements of Rudra but the god who rose to eminence in the epic period was a much more complex deity who had evolved from many local gods and their cults. The Dravidian people had a god of the animals scholars call Pasupati, who resembles Shiva and whose worship must have continued even after the arrival of the Aryans. This god was also worshipped in his phallic symbol of the lingam and this phallic worship was also absorbed into the worship of Shiva.

In the Rigveda, Rudra, the "yeller" is not a very pleasant god. He is merely a manifestation of Agni and the Maruts are his sons. In other hymns he is treated as a separate deity who is the lord of sacrifices and a healing god of animals. However, he is also an angry god, Rudra means the god who shouts. He has a red skin, a blue neck, and a thousand eyes who rides a chariot carrying a thunderbolt, bows and arrows and is "as terrible as a wild beast, destructive and fierce". At another place he is described as "dark, black, destroying, terrible". And one hymn intriguingly calls him "the bountiful, the lord of spirits and the lord of thieves".

Shiva first appears as a complete god with his own myths in the epics. In the Ramayana, Rama breaks the bow that Shiva had given to King Janaka and wins Sita as a bride. Then even though he is an avatar of Vishnu he worships Shiva just before crossing the ocean to invade Lanka. The Mahabharata has passages that call Vishnu supreme and others that praise Shiva as Mahadeva, the great god. It must have been a time of strife between the devotees of the two deities because the epic is full of mutual claims of superiority. Also there are more conciliatory passages by writers saying that in the final analysis Shiva and Vishnu are the same. One passage in the

Harivamsa trying to reconcile the two warring sects says, there is "no difference between Shiva who exists in the form of Vishnu and Vishnu who exists in the form of Shiva".

The Matsya, Kurma, Linga, Shiva, Skanda, and Agni puranas are all written in the praise of Shiva and his myths are found in them. Many of the myths show a conflict between Shiva and the other gods in which he comes out supreme. He cuts off one of the heads of Brahma after an argument. At the churning of the sea of milk Vishnu prays to him to rescue the earth from the poison flowing out of the mouth of the snake Vasuki. Once when he was meditating, Kama the god of love, had ignited passion in Parvati and she had disturbed her husband's meditation. At this Shiva's third eye had opened and poor Kama was burnt to ashes. However, Shiva was calmed by Parvati's entreaties and revived Kama.

Shiva the destroyer is called Mahakala, the great time and the fearsome Bhairava and when he dances the Tandava, he is Nataraja, the Lord of the Cosmic Dance. However, in Hindu belief, destruction and creation are part of the same cycle, so Shiva or Shankara is also auspicious as he begins the new cycle of creation. The Shiva lingam is the symbol of this creative force of Shiva and his phallic symbol is worshipped more often than his images. The lingam combined with the female organ of the yoni, the female creative force of shakti, symbolises all that is creative in the universe.

The appearance of the first lingam is told in a myth of the jyotirlingam, the lingam of effulgent light. The story begins when Brahma, Vishnu, and Shiva could not agree about who among the three was the supreme god. So they consulted the Vedas for an answer and all the four Vedas said that Shiva was supreme. Both Brahma and Vishnu were reluctant to accept their verdict at which volatile Shiva lost his temper and turned into an endless glittering column of light that pierced the sky, the earth and the netherworld.

Both Brahma and Vishnu were curious to find out where this column ended. Vishnu turned himself into a boar and dug deep into the earth while Brahma flew up to the sky on the back of his swan. They travelled for a thousand years and still could not discover the ends of the column. When they returned to earth, the column reduced in size to that of a Shiva lingam and Vishnu worshipped it as Shiva. However, Brahma claimed that he had seen the end of the column and he called to a ketaki flower to bear false witness and support his claim. At which Shiva finally lost his patience and turned into the raging Bhairava and cut off one of the five heads of Brahma.

Now there is no greater sin than the killing of a Brahmin and so the skull of Brahma's severed head stuck to Shiva's hand and would not come off. Shiva performed many penances and visited many pilgrimages but could not free himself from it until he arrived at Varanasi where his penances were successful and the skull fell off. This is why Varanasi or Kashi is Shiva's favourite city on earth. Here Shiva is the supreme god and all the other gods worship him. Created from pure light, the jyotirlingams are called Swayambhu or self created. There are twelve jyotirlingams in the country and among them the most sacred are at Kedarnath, Rameshwaram, and Varanasi.

Varanasi or Kashi, the resplendent city of light is like a living shrine to Shiva. Every lane and corner has temples dedicated to the god and there are myriad myths that speak of Shiva's love for Kashi. It is said that after Shiva married Parvati he was looking for an abode on earth and his eyes fell on Kashi with its golden spires and he chose to stay there. Kashi is called Anandavana, his garden of bliss and as he never forsakes it, Kashi is also Avimuktaka.

The mountain dweller Shiva found a city home in Kashi and the three most sacred lingams here are of Vishveshwara, Omkareshwara, and Kedareshwara. At Kashi, Shiva offers salvation to his devotees. He himself acts as the boatman taking their souls across the ford between this world and the next. As he rows with the soul on its journey to liberation or Nirvana, he intones the Taraka mantra of salvation. This is why Kashi is the greatest tirthasthana of all, a place of pilgrimage for the Hindus.

Brahma after losing his fifth head became Chaturanana while Shiva is at times depicted with five heads as Panchanana. His five faces illustrate his five cosmic functions of creation, conservation, destruction, incarnation, and liberation. Each has a different expression and together they capture both his accessible and obscure nature. First there is Shrishti, the face of creation, and then Sthiti, the face of preservation. The angry face of destruction is called Samhara. The fourth is of the Shiva who is hard to discover, as he is concealed as Tirobhava. Finally there is the indescribable fifth face of revelation, salvation, and compassion called Anugraha.

Shiva is the Mahayogi, the great ascetic and lives the life of a nomadic mendicant, wandering in cremation grounds covered in ash, wearing a garland of skulls, accompanied by ghosts and goblins. His devotees often practise the system of meditation called yoga. He is Digambara, the naked or sky clad and Dhurjati, with matted hair. He takes intoxicating drugs and drinks and as he dances, snakes writhe around his blue throat. So he is Nilkantha, the blue necked. But this terrible face does not repulse his devotees to whom he still looks hypnotically handsome. This aspect of Shiva appeals to the dark, fearful side of the human mind, where nightmares lurk. The Indian sadhus with their tridents and begging bowls are living images of the Mahayogi.

Shiva's rather unique garments have also gathered their own myths. Once when the great yogi was wandering in the forest he came upon the ashrams of rishis and here the wives of the rishis fell in love with the handsome ascetic. Angered by this, the rishis conjured up a tiger to attack him but as the tiger sprang, Shiva killed it with the nail of his little finger, stripped off his skin and wore it around his body. The rishis sent serpents and he wrapped them around his throat like garlands. A wild elephant was stripped of his skin and Shiva now had a cloak around his shoulders. Finally a demon dwarf, apasmara, was unleashed on him and Shiva danced on it and it forever stayed under his foot. Then the rishis understood who stood before them and worshipped him.

Many of the myths portray Shiva as an outsider in the assembly of gods and this reflects the time when the worship of the non-Vedic Shiva was still being resisted by the priesthood. Shiva and the Devi were deities of the people whose popularity forced the priesthood to admit them into the Hindu pantheon. Even today Shiva's simple rituals of worship and symbols reflect his non-Vedic, Dravidian beginnings. Among all the myths the one around Daksha's sacrifice illustrates this stage of transition the most clearly, as the Vedic gods first accept and then are eclipsed by the power of Shiva.

The story of Daksha's great sacrifice first appears in the Brahmanas. Daksha was a son of Brahma and as a Prajapati, one of the fathers of the human race. Among his many daughters was the beautiful Sati who chose to marry Shiva. This did not please Daksha as Shiva was hardly the ideal groom for his daughter but obeyed Brahma who wanted the marriage to take place. The Vedic gods lived like kings in palaces, travelled in chariots, wore jewels and silks, while Shiva could only offer a mountain home and the life of a wandering ascetic. However, Sati was adamant and Daksha allowed her to marry Shiva.

Daksha was angered even more when at a gathering of the gods all the others got up to greet him except Brahma and Shiva, who both remained seated. Brahma as his father was rightfully waiting to be greeted by him but Shiva's actions were taken as an insult by Daksha. So when Daksha decided to hold a big sacrifice he invited every god in heaven except Shiva. Sati saw the chariots of the gods all heading for the sacrifice and in spite of Shiva asking her not to, insisted on going to Daksha's home.

At the sacrifice Daksha explains his not inviting Shiva to the assembly of gods in these words, "What is his lineage and what is his clan? What place does he belong to and what is his nature? What does he do for a living and how does he behave? This fellow who drinks poison and rides a bull. He is not an ascetic, for how can one who carries a weapon be an ascetic? He is not a householder for he lives in the cremation ground. He is not a celibate student, for he has a wife. And he cannot be a forest dweller, for he is drunk with the conceit of his lordship."

Daksha goes on painting Shiva as being outside the order of caste and therefore undeserving of worship, "He is not a Brahmin for the Vedas do not know him as one. Since he carries a spear and trident he might be a kshatriya but he is not. Since he delights in the destruction of the world, he cannot be a kshatriya, who protects the world from harm. And how can he be a vaishya, for he never has any wealth? He is not even a shudra, for he wears the snake as a sacred thread. So he is beyond the castes and the stages of life," and so it goes on, describing an interloper into the pantheon of Vedic gods.

On the day of the sacrifice Sati discovered that her husband was missing from the gathering. Hurt and insulted she jumped into the yajna fire and died. Hearing of her death an enraged Shiva appeared at the gathering with his matted locks flaring around his head like flames. From these locks two demons appeared, Virbhadra and Bhadrakali and they immediately destroyed the sacrifice and attacked the gods. They cut off Daksha's head, knocked out Pushan's teeth, Bhrigu lost all his hair and they plucked out Bhaga's eyes. As chaos reigned Vishnu intervened and persuaded the gods to worship Shiva. As his anger cooled, Shiva allowed Daksha to live but with the head of a goat. Later Sati would be reborn as Parvati, the daughter of the Himalayas and his wife Mena and after many penances Parvati would once again win Shiva as her husband.

Shiva is also involved in the descent of the Ganga river to earth. In the beginning Ganga was a goddess and a celestial river that flowed in heaven. On earth there ruled a mighty king named Sagara who performed a grand Ashvamedha Yajna that rivalled those that were performed by the gods. The gods became jealous of Sagara's growing power and when the sacred horse of the sacrifice was sent out to wander the land, Indra hid the horse. As the horse did not return, Sagara sent his sixty thousand sons to search for it. In their quest they dug so deep into the earth that the oceans were created and that is why they are called Sagara. During their searches in a forest they disturbed a sage, Rishi Kapila at his meditations. The angered rishi burnt Sagara's sons to ashes.

The ashes of the sons lay at the bottom of the ocean and the only way their souls could be freed was for Ganga to descend to earth to wash them away with her sacred waters. However, as a goddess she refused to come to earth and the penances of Sagara failed to persuade her. Many years later Bhagirath, a descendent of Sagara performed the severest of austerities and Ganga was forced to answer his prayers. But she was still unwilling and in her rage she flowed down in a fierce, angry torrent.

The gods feared that her turbulent waters would engulf the earth and kill all living creatures. They all prayed to Shiva to save the earth and he obligingly put his head in the path of the angry river. He caught her waters in the coils of his hair and she wandered there for a long while until Shiva allowed her to flow out divided into seven streams. These streams flowed down the Himalayas and the Ganga became the life giving river of the people. The ashes of Sagara's sons were purified at Ganga Sagar on the Bay of Bengal and they finally gained liberation. So Shiva wears two embellishments in his hair—the Ganga and the moon that he had picked up during the churning of the sea of milk.

Shiva is always linked with Shakti—the female power of the Mother Goddess, the Devi. So in our mythology, among all the gods, it is the mendicant Shiva who is portrayed as a family man with a wife and children. Shiva is married to Parvati, one aspect of the Devi who is called by many names—Uma, Annapurna, Jagaddhatri, Durga and Kali. And like her consort, the Devi is also a goddess with many faces. She can be the generous, food bearing Ma Annapurna and the fierce warrior goddess like Durga.

Shiva and Parvati's two sons are Kartikeya, who is the general of the army of the gods and Ganesha, the benign elephant headed deity of good fortune. This family stays at Mount Kailash but when the wanderlust hits Shiva and he wanders among the ghosts and goblins in cremation grounds he is accompanied by his two companions Nandi and Bhringi. Nandi is also the bull that is Shiva's chosen vehicle.

It is Parvati who is responsible for Shiva's third eye. Once when Shiva was meditating on Mount Kailash, Paravati crept up from behind and playfully covered his eyes. Immediately the sun went out and darkness descended on the three worlds and all life was threatened. But before creation could be destroyed, a third eye burst out of Shiva's forehead and light was restored but its rays were so fierce that the Himalayas were burnt to ashes. Parvati had to beg for forgiveness from Shiva before he restored her father to life.

Merciful Shiva is also very generous with his boons. Many times demons like Hiryanakasipu and Ravana earned boons from him that put the gods in danger. He gave the Pasupata weapon to Arjuna and the battle axe to Parashuram. Yudhishthira received a weapon called Shakta, Janaka got a bow, and Rama powerful arrows. When Arjuna went looking for him, Shiva came disguised as a hunter, Kirata and challenged Arjuna to a duel. He defeated Arjuna and then revealed himself and gave him the powerful Pasupata.

There are many myths of Shiva killing demons but the most interesting is the ambivalent relationship between Shiva and the rakshasa king Ravana. The demon king of Lanka was a scholar who meditated on Shiva for a long time to gain the power to defeat the gods. There is even a hymn to Shiva that is said to have been composed by Ravana. Shiva, always easily pleased, blessed Ravana and granted his request. However, this made him so arrogant that he challenged Shiva himself.

One day Ravana stood below Mount Kailash and called out a challenge to Shiva but the god ignored him. At this Ravana raised the mountain by the strength of his arms, trying to topple Shiva from it. Parvati was full of fear but Shiva just used the toe of one foot to hold the mountain in place. Shiva pressed down so hard that Ravana's arms were crushed under the weight of the mountain and he began to scream in pain. Shiva let him yell for one thousand years and then released him after Ravana had begged for mercy. In this way the demon king got his name of Ravana, the crier.

Shiva's greatest festival is Shivaratri, "The Night of Shiva" when he is worshipped with all-night prayers at his temples. Shiva is said to have married Parvati on this moonless Amavasya night when he also dances the Tandava. There are temples to Shiva everywhere in India but some of them carry a greater sacredness. The most important Shaiva pilgrimage is the city of Varanasi (Kashi) which is said to be his favourite place on earth. Here many lingams are claimed to be the first jyotirlingam and among them is the one at the Kashi Vishwanatha Temple, the most important temple to Shiva. The Pallava kings built temples to the god at Kanchipuram, like the magnificent Kailasanatha Temple, and the Chola king Raja Raja built the Brihadishvara Temple at Thanjavur in Tamil Nadu. Shiva's most sacred temple in the Himalayas is at Kedarnath and devotees worship also at the remote Kailash Mountain. The temple at Rameshwaram in Tamil Nadu is sacred because Rama worshipped Shiva here with a lingam made by Sita with sand. The Elephanta Cave Temple in Maharashtra has some of the greatest sculptures of Shiva in his many aspects, including the majestic three-headed Mahadeva figure. The classical dances, especially Bharatanatyam, often portray Nataraja, the dancer and there are musical ragas like Bhairav and Shankara that are sung in his praise.

The icons of Shiva show him in a multitude of moods and the sculptors of South India have a special affinity to Shiva. The most famous depiction of Shiva is as Nataraja, the lord of the dance, its finest examples being the Chola bronzes. Shiva stands with one foot raised in a fluid movement of dancing, his hair flowing out like a halo around his head. One hand holds the damaru, the other a deer, the third a ball of fire, and the fourth points to his foot that rests

on Apasmara, the dwarf of ignorance. The figure is circled
by an aureole of flames. Nataraja is the patron god of Indian
classical dance and at his temple at Chidambaram all the
postures of Bharatanatyam are carved on the walls of the
gateways.

In his image called the Kalyana Sundara Murti, Shiva is
a handsome young ascetic the women fall in love with, and
as the mystic poet Mahadeviakka sings,

> My husband comes home today
> Wear your best, wear your jewels
> The Lord, white as jasmine,
> Will come anytime now,
> Girls, come, meet Him at the door.

As Tripurantaka he is the divine archer who destroyed
three demon cities with just one arrow. As Hari-Hara, half
his body is of Shiva and the other of Vishnu. While as the
androgynous Ardhanariswara, the other half is of Shakti,
carved with all the womanly curves and soft contours. As
Somaskanda he sits with Parvati, both dressed like royalty,
with their son Kartikeya in the middle. At times Shiva's
image is shown within a lingam as Shiva Lingodbhava and
his five faces form a lingam in the Mukhalinga. As Jnana
Dakshinamurti he is the handsome young teacher, sitting with
one leg crossed over the other, his hair framing a calm,
compassionate face and his right hand raised in the posture
of teaching.

Shiva has one thousand and one names that are recited
like a mantra by his devotees. He is Shankara, the auspicious

and tranquil, Gangadhara, the bearer of the Ganga; Chandra Sekhara, the moon crested and Girisha, the lord of the mountains; Mahakala, the great time; Ishana, the ruler, Kedara, who lives in the mountains and Pasupati, the lord of the animals; Shambhu, the auspicious; Mahesha, the great lord and Vishwanatha, the lord of the world; Tryambaka, the three-eyed; Hara, the seizer and Aghora, the terrible; Bhuteshwara, the lord of the ghosts; Vyomkesa, with hair like the sky and Ashutosh, who is easily pleased. Shiva is also Rudra, the yeller, Nilalohit, the blue-red god; Diptani, the shining and Kasinath, the lord of Kashi.

CHAPTER TEN

The Devi

Parvati—Uma—Gauri—Durga—Chandika—Kali
For the ignorant you are the island city of the sun
For the mentally stagnant, a waterfall of nectar
Flowing from a bouquet of intelligence
For the poor you are a rosary of wishing jewels
　　　　　　　— Praise of the Devi in Saundarya Lahari

The Devi, simply means the goddess and the Hindus have
imagined her as a kind and giving mother and also as a strong,
at times ruthless fighter. So like her many faces, the Devi has
many names, ranging from the benevolent Parvati to the
beautiful, golden skinned Gauri and the dark and ferocious
Kali. The goddess is the fecund earth and a symbol of fertility
and she is also the divine force, the shakti of the powers
of Shiva.

In the beginning the goddess was worshipped as the
consort of a number of gods as they were the shakti, the
divine strength and cosmic power of their spouses. A god was

visualised as inactive and transcendent and it was the goddess who was active and immanent. Somehow it is as the consort of Shiva that the Devi gained the most prominence and with it the maximum number of myths. The generous but reclusive Shiva allowed his consort to capture the limelight when it came to the important business of killing demons. The icon of the Ardhanariswara, half Shiva and half Shakti is a graphic portrayal of this union of divine forces.

The worship of the Devi is intimately intertwined with the worship of Shiva. For instance, in South India, Shiva is believed to be a passive force that is energised only when he is combined with the active shakti of the goddess they call Amman. And so every temple to Shiva has its separate shrine dedicated to the Amman. She is often portrayed with the physical characteristics that also belong to Shiva. Durga also has a third eye, she wields the trishula, the trident and at times she has matted hair and like Shiva possesses a destructive and angry face. Both Shiva and the Devi have the Ugra roop, the angry persona and the Saumya roop, the benign persona and this is unique to these two enigmatic deities.

The worship of the Devi, especially as Durga and Kali is the most prevalent in Eastern India, in Bengal, and Assam. Here the warrior goddess receives devotions in her own temples and has her own festivals where Shiva is just a token presence. The Devi is mother and protector who even has a family that comes down to earth with her and it is in Bengal that one finds books of praise and hymns composed for her. One of the finest poets who wrote on the Devi as Kali was Ramprasad and his hymns are sung even today,

O Kali! You danced in a sea of blood
Now you are fond of the waters of the Yamuna
Prasada laughs, immersed in inner bliss and says,
O Mother, I have fathomed the mystery after reflection
Krishna, Kali and Shiva—all are one
I have known, O Lady.

There was the worship of a Mother Goddess in the Indus Valley Civilization but the Aryan-Vedic pantheon had little place for a powerful goddess. There was Prithivi, the earth goddess; Aditi, the mother of the Adityas; Ushas, the goddess of dawn; Aranyani, the goddess of forests, but it was the male gods like Indra, Surya, and Agni who received praise and oblations. However, like the worship of Shiva, the cult of the Mother Goddess never really abated and it rose to prominence during Puranic times. Both Shiva and the Devi forced their way into the Vedic pantheon because the priesthood could not deny their popularity. So by the time of the epics, warriors like Rama and Arjuna are shown worshipping her and praying to her for victory and it is Krishna, the supreme Vishnu Avatar, who tells Arjuna to ask for Durga's blessings. The Devi was obviously too influential to be ignored and as a warrior goddess she literally fought her way to a place in the Hindu pantheon.

The myths of the Devi in her many faces like Durga, Kali or Parvati are found in the Markandeya Purana, the Devi Bhagavad, the Chandi Mahatmaya, Shiva, and Vamana puranas. The Devi appears initially as the consort of the important gods. Saraswati is Brahma's divine companion, Lakshmi rises from the sea of milk and flies to sit beside

Vishnu and Parvati is merely Shiva's wife, living on Mount Kailash. Then gradually the Devi gained her own band of devotees for whom she as a deity deserved their exclusive worship and her character began to widen, encompassing many aspects of a many faceted goddess.

There was the cult of the Matrikas, the Great Mother, who were in early myths the female emanations of male gods and then grew to assume independent personalities. The Saptamatrikas, the seven great devis, are the consorts of the gods like Brahmani of Brahma, Vaishnavi of Vishnu, Bhairavi of Shiva. Then in the esoteric Tantrik worship of the Devi she acquired a total of ten personae, the Mahavidyas of Kali, Tara, Shodashi, Bhuvaneshwari, Chhinnamasta, Bhairavi, Dhumavati, Bagala, Matangi, and Kamala.

As the many mythologies of the world show, the Mother Goddess is a powerful presence everywhere. From Isis in Egypt to Ishtar of Babylon and Cybele of the Greeks, there are influential goddesses with their own cults and myths. Of these Ishtar and Cybele are also depicted riding chariots pulled by lions. In India even heterodox sects like Jainism and Buddhism could not resist the power of the cult of the goddess. One of the Mahavidyas, Tara, also became the merciful goddess and saviour of the Buddhists and is worshipped in Tibet. For the Jains, Saraswati, the goddess of speech and learning, is a very important deity.

The earliest appearance of the Devi in myths is in the Puranic story of Sati, the daughter of Prajapati Daksha who married Shiva and then killed herself because Shiva had not been invited to an important yajna by her father. (*see*: chapter on Shiva) Another version of the myth explains the location

of the places of pilgrimage of the Devi called Pithasthanas—
the places where pieces of the body of Sati fell and the Devi
has temples dedicated to her worship. One of the most
famous is the Kalighat Temple in Kolkata where one of her
toes is said to have fallen.

In this version, once Shiva heard of the death of Sati he
entered the place of the sacrifice in a rage and as his demons
demolished everything, he found Sati's lifeless body lying
beside the altar. Mad with grief he picked up her body and
began to dance the Tandava, the terrible dance of destruction
that ends existence on earth. The gods had no way of
stopping him and prayed to Vishnu to come to their aid.
Vishnu knew that no one, not even he, could stop Shiva when
he was in this violent state and he had to find a way to cool
his anger. He realised that as long as Shiva was carrying Sati's
body his grief would burn and he wouldn't stop dancing. So
he followed Shiva and using his Sudarshana Chakra he cut
Sati's body into fifty-one pieces. Once he no longer felt the
weight of Sati's body, Shiva's agony abated and he calmed
down and the earth was thus saved.

Sati was destined to be the eternal consort of Shiva and
in her next birth she was born as the daughter of the
Himalaya and his wife Mena. In this birth she was called
Parvati and Uma. A pampered child of the god of the
mountains, Parvati lived a life of carefree comfort until one
day she saw Shiva meditating in the hills. Since the death of
Sati he had immersed himself in the deepest contemplation
and was not even aware of the world around him and Parvati
fell in love with this handsome ascetic. She came every day
to his meditation spot, carrying flowers and fruits, she swept

the place and placed a bowl of fresh water beside him but Shiva did not even know of her existence.

Meanwhile an asura named Taraka was becoming a nuisance to the gods and the sages and they asked for Brahma's help. Brahma told the gods that the only one who was destined to kill Taraka was the son of Shiva and Parvati. The problem was that in spite of Parvati's devotion Shiva showed no interest in her. So the gods decided to help Paravati's cause and came down to earth. Though it was the deepest winter with snow lying on Mount Kailash, Vasanta, the god of spring turned the hill into a green orchard and a fragrant flower garden. Then Kama, the god of love prepared his flower arrows and ready to strike Shiva, he lay in wait near the place where Shiva sat meditating.

The next day Parvati came to the hills and was amazed to see the leafy trees and blooming flowers. She gathered the fruits and flowers and as she laid them at Shiva's feet her hands touched him. Immediately Kama let fly his arrow that woke Shiva from his trance. But instead of falling in love with Parvati, he was so furious with Kama that his third eye opened and poor, well-meaning Kama was burnt to ashes. A despondent Parvati returned home to find a wailing Rati, the wife of Kama, mourning her dead husband. Brahma reassured her that the day Shiva and Parvati were wed, Kama would once again come back to life.

Now with Kama's life at stake, Parvati was even more determined to win Shiva and began the severest of penances. She went into the forest and as she meditated in the severest winter she stood in the icy waters of a Himalayan river. In summer she sat surrounded by four fires. She ate nothing, growing thin and weak and she was called Aparna because she would not even eat a single leaf to sustain herself. Her mother Mena gave her the name of Uma when she saw Parvati's penances and exclaimed in distress, "U Ma !" and begged her to stop. But Shiva still refused to answer her prayers.

Then one day a handsome young ascetic came to her and after watching her praying wondered if a god like Shiva was worth so much pain and trouble. He was just a penniless mendicant, living on a hill under trees and wearing animal skins. What did Parvati see in him? Wouldn't it be easier for her to go back to her happy life in her parent's home? An angry Parvati refused to listen to him at which the ascetic revealed himself to be Shiva. When the two were married, as Brahma had predicted, Kama came back to life and their first child was Kartikeya who grew up to kill the demon Taraka.

Parvati is always portrayed as a wife sitting beside Shiva. Her sons are Kartikeya and Ganesha and in Bengal, Lakshmi and Saraswati are called her daughters. Parvati is dark skinned, but has a golden skinned persona called Gauri. It is said that once Shiva teased her and called her Kali, dark skinned, and deeply hurt she went into the forest and refused to return. At which an apologetic Shiva took her to the river Ganga where after a bath when Parvati appeared again she had become the golden skinned Gauri.

The triad of Sati-Parvati-Uma is the benign wife-mother-provider aspect of the Devi. But her devotees also look for another role from their goddess, as a fierce fighter, wielder of mighty weapons and at times a ferocious, merciless presence on the battlefield. Durga-Chandika-Kali encompass this active, at times darker aspect of the Devi. These three are also the consorts of Shiva but do not live in the hills like Parvati. Durga as Vindhyavasini is often shown to live in the Vindhya hills. Kali is purely a presence in the battlefield and as Bhairavi in cremation grounds and with Chandika she is only absorbed in the destruction of the asuras.

Another thing that is different about the warrior goddesses is that unlike Sati or Parvati they have not been given parents. They were created through the divine emanation of the gods, they were the shakti or primal energy of the gods and only appeared when there was the need for a goddess of war. The first such warrior Devi was Durga, the others like Chandika and Kali are really fiercer aspects of her more benign face. Also it is Durga, seated on the lion who epitomises the Devi and is worshipped across the country. The Shaktya cults of Kali and Chandika are to be found more in the east, especially Bengal, where Durga has the most important festival but it is Kali who receives the daily puja at innumerable temples.

Parvati earned the name of Durga when she took a militant form to slay an asura called Durgam. Another explanation for the name is given by Vishnugupta Chanakya, the Mauryan chief minister, who believed that Durga was the goddess who protected a fortress, a durg, and he suggested that all forts should have a temple dedicated to her. Durga really enters centrestage with the long battle to slay the asura of many faces and forms called Mahisha who had vanquished all the gods in heaven.

The Markandeya Purana tells the tale of Durga Mahishamardini. Mahishasura was a demon who had performed austerities for many years and had gained a boon from Brahma. He asked for the power to be able to change his form at will and become invincible in battle, whom no one could kill. Unable to refuse a boon he had already promised, a reluctant Brahma said that no male—god or man or asura would succeed in killing Mahisha. The asura king then attacked the gods and there was a terrific battle between the gods and the demons that went on for hundreds of years but the demons were triumphant. The asuras then invaded and occupied Indra's heaven Amravati and the gods had to come down and hide on earth.

As the three worlds shook with the oppression of the asuras, Mahisha decided to test his powers. He transformed himself into a beautiful woman, entered the ashram of Rishi Kattayana, and then destroyed the rishi's sacrifice. Kattayana recognised Mahisha and said in anger that as he had come disguised as a woman, it would be a woman who would kill him. The asura, drunk with power, only laughed at the rishi's curse.

The gods knew that only their combined energies in the form of a goddess could defeat Mahisha. They all gathered at one place and then a dazzling effulgence flowed out of them to form a figure of incomparable beauty and majestic power. She was the first Shakti, Adi Shakti and called Durga. Her face came from the shakti of Shiva, Yama's power gave her the dark cloud of long hair, Vishnu created her ten hands. Chandra, the moon, Indra and Varuna formed different parts of her body. Brahma's power resided in her feet, Surya her toes and Agni opened her three lotus eyes.

As the figure of this golden goddess reached up to the sky, her glow surrounded her and the gods knew that Mahisha had met her match. The Chandi Mahatmaya describes this magnificent goddess as "wearing anklets around her lotus like feet, a jewelled belt, clothes encrusted with gems and a necklace of pearls. She is blue skinned with three eyes and carries weapons in her hundred hands".

Now Durga had to be armed with the most powerful weapons and each god presented her with his own. She received Shiva's trident, the Trishula; Vishnu's discus, the Sudarshana Chakra and Brahma's rudraksha prayer beads and Kamandalu bowl. Varuna gave her his conch shell to blow before the battle and his noose, the Pasha. Agni's gift was a dart, Vayu's a bow and Surya's a quiver of arrows. Indra handed her his thunderbolt, the Vajra; Kuvera a mace, Kala a sword and shield and Vishwakarma his battle axe. The gods also offered her a choice of the mounts to ride, including Indra's Airavat elephant and Vishnu's Garuda bird but Durga chose to ride Himalaya's lion.

A resplendent Durga rode into battle at the head of her army, blowing on her conch and playing her battle drums and when she twanged at the strings of her bow it sounded like a threatening roll of thunder. Mahisha first sent his two generals Chiksura and Chamara at the head of his army and Durga easily vanquished Chiksura while the lion was enough to defeat Chamara. Then Mahisha appeared to fight and every time Durga attacked him he would change his form to confuse her. He appeared as a lion and when Durga cut off his head a giant carrying a sword came out of the lion. As the giant was killed Mahisha changed into an elephant and rampaged through Durga's army.

Durga realised that the moment she struck Mahisha he changed his form and so did not die. As she strengthened herself with draughts of Soma, Shiva told her that the only way to kill Mahisha would be to strike exactly at the moment when he was changing from one form to the next. Then as Mahisha attacked Durga in the form of a giant buffalo she used her battle axe to cut off his head. Then as Mahisha himself began to appear from the bloody neck, at the point when only his upper half had formed and the lower half was still that of a buffalo, Durga put a foot on his shoulder and pierced his heart with the trident.

The Bengali festival of Durga Puja held every autumn in the month of Kartik celebrates the creation, battle and victory of Durga. She was created by the gods on Mahalaya day, she is worshipped on Saptami, Ashtami, and Navami. She is said to have killed Mahishasura on Dashami. In Bengal a popular belief has also turned these days into a time when Durga and her family come to earth to visit her parents. She is accompanied by Lakshmi, Saraswati, Kartikeya, and Ganesha, who are her children. The earthen image shows her as a resplendent goddess armed with weapons killing the half asura half buffalo demon but in an odd contrast she is also surrounded by her family.

This period is celebrated in the north as Dussehra as this is also the time when Rama prayed to Durga before he invaded Lanka. Ravana was killed on Dussehra day which coincides with the Dashami of Durga Puja when Mahisha was also slain. These nine days of Navaratri are the time for the worship of the goddess in her many forms. This is when she received worship not just from people but also the gods and even Rama who was an avatar of Vishnu. Navaratri is one of the most auspicious periods of the year.

The worship of Durga takes in her ten main aspects that are called Dasa Mahavidyas. She is Durga, Dasabhuja, the ten armed; Singhavahini, riding a lion; Mahishasurmardini, the slayer of Mahisha; Jagadhatri, mother of the world; Kali, the black one; Muktakesi, with open hair; Tara, the benevolent one; Chinnamasta, the one with a cut head; and Jagadgauri, the Gauri of the world. The Dasa Mahavidyas are worshipped in the unorthodox Yogic cult of Tantra and sometimes include other aspects called Shodashi, Bhuvaneshwari, Bhairavi, Dhumavati, Bagala, Matangi, and Kamala.

Among the ten it is Chandika-Kali who has acquired a rounded persona that often leads to the worship of a deity and with it she has gathered her own myths. The most important being her long battle against the asura brothers Shumbha and Nishumbha. As found in the Chandi Mahatmaya, it is one of the most rousing tales of a battle with dramatic scenes of conflict, strategy and triumph. It begins in the same pattern as the other myths with the two asuras gaining a boon from Brahma that no male—god or human would be able to defeat them. The gods are defeated once again by Shumbha and Nishumbha and Indra loses his heaven. Shumbha begins to rule there as the gods are forced to come down to earth to pray to the goddess.

As the gods prayed by the banks of the Ganga, the Devi appeared before them as the beautiful Chandika and promised to help. She went up to heaven and began to wander around Indra's heaven where she was seen by Chanda and Munda, two servants of Shumbha-Nishumbha. The two hurried back to their masters with the news of this golden goddess of incomparable beauty and they said she deserved to be the consort of one of the asura kings.

Shumbha and Nishumbha then sent their messenger named Sugreeva to Chandika with an offer. She could choose one of the brothers and become the queen of heaven. Chandika listened patiently and then said she would have been delighted to accept the offer except for one problem. She had taken a vow that she would only marry someone who could defeat her in battle. Hearing her reply the asura brothers were furious and sent their commander of the army, Dhumralochan, with orders to bring the goddess to them, dragging her by her hair. It was after all quite beneath them to fight a mere woman.

Dhumralochan and his army arrived to discover Chandika sitting on her lion smiling a gentle welcome. He decided he could handle her alone and went rushing towards her to grab her by the hair. Dhumralochan had only come half way when he was burnt to ashes by Chandika's fiery breath and then her lion wrecked such havoc among the asuras that they all ran away.

Shumbha-Nishumbha still thinking it beneath them to fight a female next sent Chanda and Munda with a larger army. Coming face to face with Chandika, Chanda sent off such a shower of arrows that the sky darkened and Munda aimed flying darts by the thousand at Chandika. The goddess now became angry, her face darkened and her skin turned black. From her forehead appeared a terrible apparition called Kali. This goddess of pure shakti wore the skin of a tiger as a skirt and a necklace of skulls around her neck. She carried a curved scimitar called a kharga and a giant snake and strode out to battle with her tongue lolling out, hungry for blood.

As Chanda and Munda watched horrorstruck, Kali began to grow before their eyes until her immense figure touched the sky. Then she opened her huge mouth and began to swallow whatever came in her way—asuras, horses, chariots, weapons, and even the trees and mountains that Chanda-Munda threw at her. Then she used her snake to tie up the two asuras and dragged them to Chandika who ordered Kali to cut off their heads. Then Chandika told her that as the slayer of Chanda and Munda, Kali would also be known as the goddess Chamunda.

Finally the asura kings Shumbha and Nishumbha realised that they were not facing a mere goddess and they gathered their forces and prepared for a battle to death. The brothers would now personally lead the army and with them would be a dangerous asura the gods feared greatly named Raktaveeja. On the battlefield Raktaveeja was impossible to defeat because the moment he was wounded and drops of his blood fell to the ground more Raktaveejas appeared, until there was a perpetually growing army of these asuras.

Though Chandika was unafraid, the gods decided to create seven warrior goddesses from their own effulgence and arm them with their own weapons. These were the Sapta Matrikas, the seven goddesses of pure shakti, protective mothers and fighting furies. Shiva as Lord Maheshwar created Maheshwari and Brahma's power formed Brahmani. Vishnu's matrika was Vaishnavi, his Varaha Avatar's was Varahi and the Narasimha Avatar's was a half lioness-half woman named Narsimhi. Kartikeya created Kaumari and Indra's warrior goddess was the elephant riding Aindri.

HANUMAN
The monkey god, son of Vayu, the god of the winds.
Devoted follower of Rama.

KRISHNA

Cowherd, king and philosopher. Eighth avatar of Vishnu.
Spoke the verses of the Bhagavat Gita in the
Mahabharata.

NATARAJA
Shiva, the Puranic god of destruction in his form as
the Lord of the Cosmic Dance.

DURGA
The mother goddess, riding a Lion,
as the demons-Laying Mahishasura Mardini.

DEVI MATA
The mother goddess riding a tiger in her form as
the eight-armed Ashtabhuja Bhavani.

GANESHA
Benevolent elephant-headed god of
wisdom and good fortune. Son of Shiva and Parvati.

KARTIKEYA

Puranic warrior-god, son of Shiva and Parvati
in his form as the seven headed Skanda.

SARASWATI
Goddess of wisdom, Learning and arts.
Mother of the Vedas. Consort of Lord Brahma.

This army of fighting goddesses now flanked Chandika as she rode out to battle. As Shumbha-Nishumbha gave the battle cry, in reply Chandika blew on her conch, beat her battle drums, twanged her bow, and the final battle began. The Sapta Matrikas faced Raktaveeja and attacked him from all sides. But if Maheshwari pierced him with her trident or Varahi hit him with her sword, his blood gave birth to more Raktaveejas. The Matrikas fought fiercely but after a while they were facing thousands of Raktaveejas, each capable of producing more like himself. The battle began to get uneven and the gods were worried.

Chandika noticed what was happening and once again her anger produced the bloodthirsty form of Chamunda-Kali who rushed into battle with her cavernous, all devouring mouth opened hungrily. Chandika rode her lion beside her and faced Raktaveeja herself and told Chamunda that as she attacked the asura, Chamunda was to drink up his blood before it touched the ground. In the mighty battle that followed Raktaveeja was wounded again and again by Chandika and as Chamunda drank up all his blood, a weakened Raktaveeja crashed to the ground and died.

By now Shumbha and Nishumbha were beside themselves with rage and came rushing in to face Chandika. Nishumbha attacked Chandika's lion and wounded him. This angered her so much that she smashed his sword and shield to pieces. Nishumbha aimed his spear and then a whirling mace and both were broken in mid-air by her discus. Then Chandika cut him down with her arrows and he fell senseless to the ground. With his brother lying unconscious Shumbha now faced Chandika and taunted her for fighting him with the help of the seven matrikas. At which Chandika allowed the matrikas to merge into her body and faced Shumbha alone.

Shumbha came to fight carrying weapons in his eight arms and riding a swift chariot. He showered her with arrows and darts, swung his sword, and aimed his spear all at the same time. Chandika did not even blink, calmly destroying his chariot and fighting off the weapons. Shumbha sprang up into mid-air to attack her from the top but Chandika flew up to face him. By then Nishumbha had also come back to fight and facing them together Chandika finally used her most powerful weapons and killed them. As the asura army lay dead, the gods showered Chandika with flowers and worshipped her with hymns of praise. Then they returned to their heaven once again.

On a moonless night in autumn, when the rest of India celebrates Deepavali, Kali-Chamunda is worshipped in Bengal. Her image shows a beautiful, dark skinned woman but she wears clothes and jewellery made of skulls and human hands and carries a bloody Kharga scimitar and a snake. Her eyes are bloodshot and she stands on the chest of the recumbent figure of Shiva and her tongue hangs out. It is said that after drinking the blood of Raktaveeja she was so maddened by the battle that she could not stop her dance of destruction. The only way Shiva could stop her was by lying down in her path. As Kali stepped on his chest she realised what she had done and stuck out her tongue in shame. Passionate, impulsive Kali is also described as the first tongue of flame in a yajna fire and is in many ways the antithesis of a calm professional fighter like Durga or Chandika.

There are temples to the Devi and even to the Matrikas and the Dasa Mahavidyas all across the country. Among the most sacred are the Kali Ghat and Dakshineshwar temples in Kolkata and the Kamakshya temple in Kamrup where Kali is worshipped. There is the Meenakshi temple in Madurai and temples in Kanchipuram, Mysore, and Chidambaram in the South. The hill top shrine of Vaishno Devi near Jammu is the most popular Devi temple in the north. One of the oldest Kali images can be seen at the Kali temple inside the Amber Fort near Jaipur. The Kali image was brought here from Jessore in Bengal by Raja Man Singh during the reign of the Mughal emperor Akbar.

Like her varied and highly contrasting persona that ranges from a loving provider and mother to a merciless, bloodthirsty fighter, the Devi has many names. The Adya Shakti, the primal energy is the Uma-Sati-Parvati-Chandika-Chamunda-Kali-Durga of the myths. She is also praised as Ishani, wife of Shiva who is called Ishan; Annapurna, the provider and Girija, the mountain born. She is Rudrani, the wife of Rudra; Haimavati, daughter of the snowy mountains and Bhairavi, the terrible. Also Ambika, the mother; Vijaya, the victorious, Gauri and Kaushiki, the golden skinned and Sarva Mangala, auspicious. She is Shakhambari, the one who nourishes the world with her body; Kamakshi, the love-eyed goddess; Meenakshi, with eyes shaped like fishes, and Kapalini, the ascetic.

CHAPTER ELEVEN

Lakshmi & Saraswati

"Holding the veena in your right hand
You play the music of the Samveda.
Your white garments glowing against your skin
With your swan beside you
I am your servant Brahmananda
Let me see and worship you."

— poet Brahmananda, in praise of Saraswati

Lakshmi

As the goddess of wealth, prosperity, good harvests, and of
love, Lakshmi is one of the most popular goddesses of the
Hindus. Also called Sri, the beautiful, she is the epitome of
feminine beauty. Lakshmi is the gentle and generous provider
of riches and so every Hindu home has its shrine to her, as
do workplaces. The presence of Lakshmi brings good fortune
and when she leaves she takes fortune with her. So the radiant
Lakshmi who is easy to please is propitiated with puja and
flowers everyday.

Lakshmi the goddess does not appear in the Rigveda but the word is used to mean good fortune. We find her as the consort of Vishnu in the Vishnu Purana. She rose to the surface of the Sea of Milk during the great churning of the ocean (*see*: Kurma Avatar) and chose to sit beside Vishnu. After that in all the following avatars of Vishnu, Lakshmi came down to earth with him. When his incarnation was the dwarf Vamana Avatar, she came as Padma. With the boar incarnate of Varaha Avatar she was Kamala. With Parashuram she was Dharani, with Rama she was Sita and with Krishna she was Rukmini.

Lakshmi is depicted as a beautiful woman with soft, gentle features and golden skin. She has an air of calm and docility that is similar to the looks of Parvati or Gauri. She is clad in golden or red silk garments and wears a lot of gold jewellery including a tiara and an unfading garland of lotus blossoms. She is usually shown seated on an open lotus, with her pet owl beside her. She carries a bunch of lotus blossoms and also a pearl rosary and at times a jewel box. Two elephants flank her, pouring Ganga water over her from water vessels. She is ever youthful and like her consort Vishnu, is a compassionate, kind hearted goddess who is easy to please. Like Parvati, Lakshmi is considered the ideal wife.

Vishnu and Lakshmi are the parents of the god of love, Kama. One day when Surya's son Revanta was riding past Vishnu's heaven Vaikuntha on horseback, he caught Lakshmi's eyes. When she saw his horse she was reminded of the divine horse Uchhaishrava which also appeared during the churning of the Sea of Milk. Noticing his wife's distracted air, Vishnu asked her why she was staring at the handsome Revanta but Lakshmi did not reply. A jealous Vishnu then cursed Lakshmi that as she was so interested in a horse and its rider, she would descend to earth and be born as a mare.

Lakshmi protested at the injustice of the curse and wanted to know how she could be released from it. Realising his mistake, a remorseful Vishnu said that she would be freed from the curse when she gave birth to a son. Lakshmi then came down to earth as a mare and began the severest of austerities at the confluence of the Kalindi and Tamasa rivers. She prayed to Shiva and Parvati and when the divine couple finally answered her prayers she told them of her predicament and begged Shiva to give her a son. Instead, Shiva sent a messenger to Vishnu with the request that he should come down to earth as a horse and release Lakshmi from her predicament. Vishnu could not refuse a request from Shiva and obeyed. A son was born to Lakshmi and Vishnu who was named Kama or Madana, the god of love and he is their only child. Free of the curse Lakshmi could then return to Vaikuntha.

Lakshmi, when she resides in a king's palace is Rajyalakshmi; in a home she is Grihalakshmi. On the battlefield she is the fickle Jayalakshmi who often changes sides. As the goddess of fame she is Yasholakshmi and as Bhagyalakshmi she spreads good fortune. And the supreme ideal goddess is the great Mahalakshmi. In the north she is worshipped on Deepavali when many traditional businesses begin their new financial year. In Bengal she is worshipped on the first Purnima after Dussehra. The auspicious mark often made on the walls of Hindu homes called the Vasudhara symbolises her presence in that place.

In the South, images of Vishnu are often flanked by Lakshmi as Sridevi and the earth goddess Bhudevi. In the east Lakshmi and Saraswati are believed to be sisters, the daughters of Shiva and Parvati and some myths make them both the wives of Vishnu. The Buddhist pantheon has four similar goddesses of Sri, beauty; Shraddha, faith; Hri, modesty and Asha, hope. In ancient times the figure of Lakshmi or her symbols of the lotus or elephants were often inscribed on coins. And many traditional fables when they talk of the danger of imminent misfortune facing the characters, describe how a weeping Lakshmi leaves a home, palace or town and is replaced by Alakshmi, misfortune.

Lakshmi is called Haripriya, the beloved of Hari; Kamala and Padma, the lotus. She is also Padmalaya as she sits on a lotus; Jaladhija, ocean born and Chanchala, the fickle one. She is Jyeshtha, the elder one; Lokmata, mother of the world and Kumbhi, the goddess with the pitcher. She is Medha, the goddess of talent; Dhriti, patience and Kirti, fame.

Saraswati

Saraswati appears in the Rigveda, though as a minor goddess. In Vedic literature she is called Vak, the goddess of speech and eloquence and as Saraswati is also a sacred river. Gradually it is the first persona that evolved into the goddess of wisdom, learning, science, and music who wrote the Vedas and invented the Devanagari script that is used for Sanskrit. The Mahabharata calls her "the mother of the Vedas". However, her connection to the river remained and even today Saraswati is believed to be a legendary hidden river, one which has to be imagined like at the Triveni at Allahabad.

As the goddess of rivers, streams, and pools Saraswati is watery and beautiful. She is depicted as a slim, graceful, fair skinned woman, dressed in white, seated on a lotus with her pet swan beside her. In her four hands she holds the stringed musical instrument, the veena, a book which is the Vedas, a rosary, and the water vessel called Kamandalu. She is a scholarly and wise goddess who prefers an austere life of asceticism and meditation. Her festival of Basant Panchami announces the arrival of spring and she is specially worshipped by students, writers, musicians, and artists.

The myths around Saraswati present rather a confusing picture of her birth and marriage. One creation myth says she was created by Brahma and as she was the result of his imagination she is called Manasa Kanya. Brahma later made her his consort and the two of them created the world (see: chapter on Brahma). However, some traditions make her a consort of Vishnu, who has two other wives, Lakshmi and Ganga. Unlike the docile Lakshmi, Sarawati is a strong willed goddess with a quick temper and a mind of her own. Many myths like the one about Pushkar (see: chapter on Brahma) show her battling her creator-consort and even showering him with curses. At times Vishnu has had to intervene to save the hapless Brahma from the anger of his sharp tongued consort. And like the other independent goddesses, Chandika and Kali, she is also childless.

Once Saraswati as Vak, the goddess of speech, had an argument with Buddhi, the mind. The mind said that it was superior because unless it produced a thought and chose to express it, speech was powerless. Speech felt that even the noblest of thoughts would be lost unless she spoke them out aloud. They decided to make Brahma-Prajapati the arbiter and asked him to judge and he favoured the mind. At which Vak flew into a rage and cursed him that from then on at sacrifices he would never be able to hear his own mantras as she would not speak them. This is why during a yajna, the priest whispers the mantras dedicated to Brahma-Prajapati.

One Vaishnava myth says that in the beginning Saraswati, Lakshmi, and Ganga were all consorts of Vishnu. Both Lakshmi and Saraswati were jealous of Ganga because they believed that Vishnu preferred her to them. Lakshmi, the docile one accepted it and did not protest but Saraswati was hardly the sort to keep quiet at such an insult. One day she threatened Ganga and was about to shower her with curses when Lakshmi tried to intervene and make peace. At which an irritated Saraswati cursed Lakshmi that she would go down to earth as a plant. Finally, angered at the injustice Lakshmi cursed Saraswati that she would become a river. Not to be outdone, Saraswati then claimed that if she had to become a river then so would Ganga.

Hearing the furore of the flying curses Vishnu arrived to discover his three wives at war. An exasperated Vishnu then decided that three wives were just too many to handle, even for a powerful god like him. So he offered Saraswati to Brahma and Ganga to Shiva and only kept Lakshmi by his side. Then as Saraswati's curse could not be reversed, he predicted that Lakshmi would be born as the Tulasi plant and would be the most worshipped plant on earth.

As the wife of Brahma, Saraswati is also known as Brahmi. She is Vak, speech and Vagishwari, the goddess of speech. She is Sharada, who plays the veena; Satarupa, with a hundred forms and Savitri, like the sun.

CHAPTER TWELVE

Ganesha & Kartikeya

"Praise to Ganesha, my beloved Ganesha
The Sacred One with a single tusk
With his broad forehead decorated with vermilion
And wearing a glowing necklace of pearls."
— Swami Tulsidas 16th Century Poet,
in praise of Ganesha

Ganesha

Ganesha is the benevolent and benign god of wisdom and remover of all obstacles. As the bestower of Siddhi, success, he is one of the most beloved gods of the Hindu pantheon, adored by his devotees in spite of his elephant head and single tusk. Gentle, calm and propitious, he epitomises prudence and is also a patron of literature. In the Vedas, Ganesha began as Ganapati, lord of the Ganas, the group of minor deities who serve the angry god Rudra. Originally the Ganas were the turbulent hosts of Rudra and were usually invoked to avoid misfortune and ward off evil.

However, over the years he has become a deity with his own cult, temples, and festivals. His worshippers are called Ganapatyas and hymns to his praise are found in the Ganapati Prakarana of the Yajnavalkya Samhita and sects worshipping Ganesha had appeared by the time of the Guptas. His special festival is Ganesha Chaturthi in the month of Ashvin just after the monsoons, when giant images are worshipped, especially in Maharashtra.

Ganesha is a presence in all temples as the worship of all the gods must begin with an invocation to him. Kind and generous Ganesha is always invoked before any important work is undertaken, be it the starting of a business, the building of a house or the writing of a book or even undertaking a journey. He is the eldest son of Shiva and Parvati though some myths say that his brother Kartikeya is older. In the east, Lakshmi and Saraswati are believed to be his sisters.

Ganesha is an endearing though odd looking deity. First of course is the elephant head on a human body. Then he obviously loves food because he has a golden skinned, plump figure with a prosperous belly and is often depicted carrying a pot of sweetmeats called modakas. In his four hands he carries a conchshell, a chakra, an elephant goad, and a lotus. Sometimes he is shown reading a book or writing on a palm leaf manuscript. His elephant head, belly, and a rat as a vehicle probably mean that he was originally the deity of a tribal cult.

Ganesha is depicted as sitting in the asana pose, standing, in the sthanaka and dancing in the nritya posture. Like his parents Shiva and Parvati, he also possesses a third eye but he is not known to open the eye in anger. In him it is more

a symbol of his wisdom. Also as Shiva's child he wears a
snake like a sacred thread and is also a dancer but unlike his
volatile parent, his dance is one of joy and not destruction.

There is more than one myth to explain the anachronism
of an elephant head for the son of such good looking parents.
It is said that a son was born to Parvati after many prayers
and the gods gathered to admire the new born child. Parvati
noticed that Shani, the god of Saturn refused to look directly
at the child, keeping his gaze fixed to the ground. Parvati
insisted that he look at her son, forgetting that Shani
possessed an evil eye.

The moment a reluctant Shani looked at the baby its head
was burnt to ashes. As a frantic Parvati began to cry, Brahma
ordered Indra to go out and bring the head of the first living
creature he could find. The first creature Indra saw was
Airavat, his own elephant and he cut off its head and brought
it to Brahma who placed it on the shoulders of the child and
brought it to life. Looking at this bizarre apparition Parvati
was even more distressed and cried even louder. At which
Brahma ordained that from then on, the child would be
worshipped before all gods and he would become the most
beloved god of the people.

Another myth says that Ganesha was formed by Parvati
from the dew of her body mingled with oils and unguents.
Once when she was having a bath she left Ganesha guarding
the door with orders that he was not to allow anyone to enter.
Just then Shiva came along and found his way barred by his
stubborn son who would not let him enter. His angry glance
burnt off the head of the child and then Shiva had to face a
very angry and distressed wife. He rushed out to find a living

creature and unfortunately all he could find was a sleeping elephant.

Even Ganesha's single tusk has generated some interesting myths. When the sage Veda Vyasa was composing the Mahabharata, he needed a scribe to take down his dictation and asked Ganesha. The god was willing but he had one condition. Vyasa was not allowed to stop even for a moment or Ganesha would leave. Then the little competition began, Vyasa dictating as fast as he could as Ganesha sat bent over the manuscript his pen flying over it. At times when Vyasa ran out of breath he would say a couple of lines of very difficult words and as Ganesha pondered over their meaning or spelling, he would take a quick rest. Then Ganesha's reed pen broke but Vyasa refused to stop. At which Ganesha broke off one of his tusks and used it as a pen.

Another myth about the missing tusk again has Ganesha guarding the door while his mother Parvati is bathing. Parashuram the seventh avatar of Vishnu, came to visit and was not pleased to discover Ganesha in his way and insisted on a duel. Ganesha immediately wrapped up Parashuram with his trunk and threw him to the ground. An incensed Parashuram then aimed his battleaxe, the Pashupata at Ganesha. Recognising the axe as one given to Parashuram by his father Shiva, Ganesha did not repel it but respectfully received the blow on one tusk that was broken.

Ganesha is called Ekadanta, single tusked; Gajanana, elephant headed and Heramba, boastful. He is Lambakarna, long eared; Lambodara, with a big belly and Vigneshwara, remover of obstacles.

Kartikeya

Kartikeya, son of Shiva and Parvati is the commander of the army of the gods and after Indra their greatest warrior against the asuras. Unlike his brother Ganesha, Kartikeya is not a universally worshipped deity. He is unknown in the Vedas but as Skanda he is a full-fledged god in the epics. In the east there is a festival dedicated to him called Kartik Puja and in the South he is worshipped as Subramanya or Murugan and is a popular rural deity in Tamil Nadu. In great contrast to the calm and benign Ganesha, he is a forceful, martial god reminiscent of the deities of the Rigveda.

Kartikeya was born destined to defeat the demon Taraka (*see*: chapter on the Devi). Another version of this myth explains why he is sometimes shown as Skanda, with six heads and twelve arms. For Taraka to be defeated Shiva and Parvati had to produce a son but Shiva was meditating in a forest far away from his wife. So Agni went to him to receive his seed but it was too hot to carry and he dropped it in the Ganga. Six boys were delivered by Ganga and when she saw them Parvati was so pleased she embraced them. However, she held them so tightly that their bodies merged into one but the six heads remained.

Another myth says that the child of Ganga was fostered by the six wives of rishis called Krittikas and as each of them wanted to nurse him the child grew six heads. Brought up by the Krittikas he became known as Kartikeya and he defeated Taraka, the asura king of the three cities of Tripura. The Mahabharata admits the confusion in the parentage of Kartikeya and says, "Some say he is Maheshwar's son, some of Agni. Some say he was born of Uma, others of the Krittikas and still others of Ganga".

Kartikeya is depicted as a handsome god riding a peacock, carrying a bow and a quiver of arrows. In Bengal they say he is an eternal bachelor and his good looks are considered the ideal of male beauty. Other traditions give him a wife named Kaumari or Devasena. Subramanya's consort is called Valli. His figure as the generalissimo of the gods was used on coins by kings in ancient India. The Somaskanda carving in the South shows a boy Skanda sitting between Shiva and Parvati. The month of Kartik in autumn has the Pitripaksha, the fortnight when Hindus remember and worship their ancestors and also the period of the Navaratri with the celebration of the Durga Puja and Dussehra. Like Ganesha, who was probably a tribal elephant god, Kartikeya may have been a peacock deity later absorbed into the Shiva cult.

There is an amusing tale of a battle of wits between the brothers Ganesha and Kartikeya. The energetic Kartikeya challenged Ganesha to a race around the world and their parents were to be the judges. While Ganesha was still planning his trip, Kartikeya took off immediately on his peacock. Plump and sedentary Ganesha was not too interested in all this strenuous activity and to top it his rat could never keep up with the peacock. So he used his knowledge of books to discover all about the world and then spoke so knowledgeably about it that Shiva and Parvati were convinced that he had actually seen all these places. So when a travel weary Kartikeya returned, he discovered that his parents had already declared Ganesha to be the winner. Another version of the myth says that Ganesha walked around his parents and then declared that he had now seen the whole world.

Kartikeya is known an Shadanana, the six headed; Mahasenapati, the great commander in chief and Kumara, the divine boy. He is Shaktidhara, the spear holder; Gangaputra, the son of Ganga; Tarakajit, the vanquisher of Taraka and Rijukaya, with a straight body.

Glossary

Agni	—	Vedic god of fire
Alvar	—	Tamil Vaishnava mystic poet
Amman	—	Mother goddess
amrit	—	nectar of immortality
Arjuna	—	hero of the Mahabharata
Aryans	—	Central Asian nomadic tribes who entered India around 2500 BC.
asana	—	seated position
ashram	—	hermitage
Asuras	—	enemies of the Vedic gods
Atharvaveda	—	the fourth Veda
avatar	—	incarnation of a deity, usually of Vishnu
Bhagavat Gita	—	'Songs of the Gita', in the Mahabharata
Bhairava	—	terrible aspect of Shiva
bhakti	—	mystic devotion
Brahma	—	God of creation, of the Hindu trinity
Brahman	—	Absolute, Hindu concept of the One God
Brahmin	—	Hindu priestly class
chakra	—	Vishnu's discus
darshana	—	viewing of a temple deity
Deva	—	god
Devi	—	goddess

dharma	—	religious laws and customs
Durga	—	warrior goddess
Ganesha	—	Elephant headed god
garbagriha	—	sanctum of a temple
Garuda	—	bird vehicle of Vishnu
gopis	—	milkmaids beloved of Krishna
Indra	—	Vedic king of the gods
jyotirlinga	—	a self manifest Shivalingam
Kailasa	—	mountain home of Shiva
Kali	—	terrible aspect of the Devi
Kali Yuga	—	the fourth Hindu Age
Kalki	—	tenth incarnation of Vishnu
karma	—	action & consequence of one's past deeds
Kartikeya	—	warrior god, son of Parvati & Shiva
Krishna	—	eighth incarnation of Vishnu
kshatriya	—	the warrior class
Lakshmi	—	goddess of plenty
linga	—	phallic symbol of Shiva
Mahabharata	—	epic poem
Mahishasura	—	buffalo demon killed by Durga
mantra	—	sacred invocations
maya	—	illusion, the unreal
Meru	—	mythical mountain in the Himalayas
moksha	—	release, liberation
Nandi	—	Shiva's bull
Narasimha	—	man-lion, incarnation of Vishnu
Nataraja	—	Shiva as the Lord of the Dance
Nayanmar	—	Tamil Shaiva mystic poet
nirvana	—	enlightenment
Om	—	the most sacred syllable
Pandavas	—	five heroes of the Mahabharata
Parvati	—	aspect of Devi, consort of Shiva
puja	—	rituals of worship

Puranas	—	collection of myths & rituals
Radha	—	Krishna's lover & favourite gopi
Rama	—	incarnation of Vishnu
Ramayana	—	epic tale about Rama
Ravana	—	demon king of Lanka
Rigveda	—	the first Veda
rita	—	cosmic order of the world
rishi	—	the sages who composed the Vedas
Rudra	—	Vedic deity, prototype of Shiva
sadhu	—	ascetic, wandering mendicant
Samaveda	—	the second Veda
samsara	—	endless cycle of birth & death
Saraswati	—	goddess of learning
Shaiva	—	worshipper of Shiva
shakti	—	divine power incarnate in the Devi
shastra	—	ancient treatise on correct practice
Shiva	—	God of destruction, of the trinity
Sita	—	Rama's consort
Skanda	—	son of Siva & Parvati
soma	—	divine drink of immortality
Surya	—	the sun god
tirtha	—	a ford, Hindu pilgrimage
Vaishnava	—	worshipper of Vishnu
Valmiki	—	sage credited with writing the Ramayana
Varuna	—	Vedic god of the heavens
Vedas	—	the oldest Hindu religious texts
Vishnu	—	God of Preservation, of the Trinity
Vritra	—	Vedic demon
Vyasa	—	sage credited with writing the Mahabharata
Yajurveda	—	the third Veda
yuga	—	a Hindu age

Bibliography

The Vedic Age, Bharatiya Vidya Bhavan

The Age of Imperial Unity, Bharatiya Vidya Bhavan

The Classical Age, Bharatiya Vidya Bhavan

The Wonder That Was India, A.L. Basham

Daily Life in Ancient India, Jeannine Auboyer

Hindu Mythology, W.J. Wilkins

A Classical Dictionary of Hindu Mythology & Religion, John Dowson

The Indian Theogony, Sukumari Bhattacharji

Hindu Myths, edited by Betty Radice

Speaking of Siva, translated by A.K. Ramanujan

The Azhwars. For the Love of God, translated by P.C. Sundaram

Chandi Mahatmaya, Bengali translation

Larousse Encyclopedia of Mythology

The Rig Veda, translated by J.K. Trikha, Bharatiya Vidya Bhavan

The Presence of Siva, Stella Kramrisch

Mahabharata, translated by Rajshekhar Basu

The Songs of the Bhagavad Gita, translated by Christopher Isherwood

Legends of the Devi, Sukumari Bhattacharji

Index